Kids' Rooms

Kids' Rooms

Ideas and Projects for Children's Spaces

by Jennifer Lévy

CHRONICLE BOOKS

SAN FRANCISCO

Photos on pages 30, 58 (top left), 62 reproduced by permission from HOUSE BEAUTIFUL,
copyright © September 1998, The Hearst Corporation. All rights reserved. Photographer: Elizabeth Zechin.

Library of Congress Cataloging-in-Publication Data:

Lévy, Jennifer.
    Kids' Rooms : ideas and projects for children's spaces / by Jennifer Lévy
      p. cm.
    Includes index.
    ISBN 0-8118-2841-7 (pbk.)
    1. Children's rooms. 2. Interior decoration. I. Louie, Elaine. II. Davey, Dania. III. Title.
    NK2117.C4 L489 2001

Printed in China

Art direction by Laura Lovett
Designed by Dania Davey and Deborah Bowman
Production assistance by Suzanne Scott
Typeset in Garamond, Bernhard Gothic, Century, and Triplex Serif

Distributed in Canada by Raincoast Books
9050 Shaughnessy Street
Vancouver, British Columbia V6P 6E5

10 9 8 7 6 5 4 3 2 1

Chronicle Books LLC
85 Second Street
San Francisco, California 94105

www.chroniclebooks.com

acknowledgments

With gratitude to all of the people who have taught and inspired me in childhood and into adulthood—my family, teachers, and professional mentors. A special thanks to my editor at Chronicle Books, Leslie Jonath, who guided me through this process with energy, enthusiasm, and patience. Also my appreciation to Laura Lovett at Chronicle Books, who thoughtfully oversaw the design process. I am grateful also to Elaine Louie for the instrumental groundwork she laid for the book, and to Penelope Rowlands for her research and refinements. I must especially thank Dania Davey, who provided not only a beautiful design, but a creative partnership—her support and steady vision saw the project through from the idea stage to its fruition. My thanks also to my assistant, Kemmeo Brown, and to the many people whose generosity of spirit and time helped make the process of creating the book a fun and inspiring experience: Ace Architects; Agnes Bourne; Laura Bohn; Sasha Emerson; Fernau Hartman Architects; Marny Maslon at Lily Henry Zoe, Santa Monica, California; Cathy Smith of Goodnight Room, Berkeley, California; Alexandra Stoddard; Jessica Strand; Jill Wood and Gretchen Gibson of A Child's Eye View in Oakland, California; and many others.

And, of course, my deepest appreciation goes to all of the parents and children who allowed me to photograph their spaces—their openness, creativity, and generosity are at the heart of this book.

contents

GREAT ROOMS

introduction

I can remember the floor plan of every place I lived as a child, and the oddest details about my bedrooms: the outsize, diamond-shaped floor tiles that reminded me of a jester's costume; the blue, fish-patterned batik curtains that felt like a magic underwater world (and probably influenced my future love for snorkeling and scuba diving); the movement of light across the walls as night traffic passed below the window. Because we lived in relatively small, city apartments, my parents had to be creative about how to use the limited space. In the room I shared with my sister, for example, my father devised a clever room-partitioning system—two-sided wall units that provided a modicum of privacy and incorporated a bookcase, toy storage, and desk space for each of us.

Our play areas and our apartments changed as we did, sometimes in ways that surprised us. When my mother, who loved the theater, was going through her "Italian phase," I came home from school one afternoon to discover cardboard Roman arches installed over the entrance to the foyer. When I was ten, we moved into an apartment with a terrace—I was delighted with this city version of a backyard.

My father built me a log cabin from a kit, and we kept it on the terrace; one blustery day, I discovered that it had vanished with the wind. We found it, in several pieces but still salvageable, nineteen floors below in a tiny alleyway. You can be sure that, when he reinstalled it, he really double-checked to make sure it was anchored properly! These are just some of the experiences that made me interested in exploring the world of children's rooms.

It's telling that so many children's books are about discovering strange, magical lands. Or about finding a little cottage (or a cave or a tree house or even a boxcar) in the woods, and setting up house within it. Children long for places of their own. Yet in the twelve years I have been photographing interiors, I have noticed that, of all the rooms in a house, children's rooms receive the least amount of attention. Or, worse still, a decorator may impose an adult's view of childhood on a kid's space, making it incredible to look at, but unsatisfying to inhabit.

At home, children need to be—and feel—safe. They need an environment that both soothes and stimulates in varying degrees, and they need to feel that they have control over their landscape. Children experience their rooms in surprising ways, sometimes in ways we grown-ups can only guess at. The simplest details—choices of color, texture, and pattern—can make a world of difference in making it their own.

For *Kids' Rooms*, I turned to the experts in order to discover what makes a great child's space. I talked to art teachers, to designers, to professional colorists. I also consulted parents and, most important, children themselves. The kids' areas on the following pages combine imagination and practicality in beguiling ways. They demonstrate a range of options and ideas. They also contain a large measure of fun, something that I hope will also inspire both kids and their parents to try some of the projects—from playful, tasseled, felt curtains to neon-bright storage boxes—that follow.

Children live more fully in the present than the rest of us do. The ideas you will find in these pages are meant to enrich and enliven that present, to nourish each child's creativity, and to support childhood as a time of joy and wonder.

—Jennifer Lévy

the elements

Every interior is the sum of its parts: color, lighting, furniture. We adults delight in shifting these elements around, changing the look of our indoor spaces whenever the mood strikes. Children's rooms, however, are more complicated. We seek to reflect the personalities of our sons and daughters within their walls, even as they move, with incredible rapidity, from one phase of childhood to the next. Letting a child's personality shine through in his or her room is a subtle art. The challenge is to make the environment imaginative, safe, flexible, and fun.

In *Kids' Rooms*, I'll show you how to create unique spaces, by combining such elements as color, storage, lighting, and furniture. And I'll do this in a way that both children and parents can enjoy together, with lots of fun, creative projects, and practical tips to share. My aim is to demystify the process of decorating and design—for kids, as well as for parents. If creating a comfortable and expressive environment is a great pleasure for adults, why can't it also be one for their children?

I strongly encourage parents to enlist their children's help in designing rooms of their own. It's a great opportunity to introduce them to color combinations and the creative manipulation of space. Kids are natural-born artists, and there are numerous ways in which they can participate, whether it's by making their own switch plates or by choosing, along with their parents, the perfect shade for the walls.

COLOR

Color is joyous. Children embrace color—but not necessarily the color that we adults take for granted. In kids' eyes, the sky is more than blue—it's red, lavender, or other shades. The rainbow a child sees may burst with purple and orange; it may be entirely different from the one seen by us literal-minded adults.

Children cherish color. They love the red of a fire engine, the orange of a marmalade cat, and the yellow of a taxicab. And we choose colors for our children over and over again. Why else do we dress them in blazing-yellow rain slickers and rain boots, or in pajamas as neon-bright as Times Square? Children

These colorful tiles create an unforgettably bright
and easy-to-clean playroom floor.

brighten our lives; we respond in kind by, literally, brightening them. Take a look around a second-grade classroom and color is what you'll see—on the walls, in the rows of crayons, on the kids themselves. Their socks alone—striped, polka-dotted, or just plain turquoise—are as bright as magic markers. Left to their own devices, many children will choose the brightest colors possible. It's no wonder parents do the same for them.

"Color stimulates us, opens our senses, whets our appetite for life," says Alexandra Stoddard, an interior designer and author. "Colors change your mood, lift your spirits, make you feel vital." When it comes to decorating a child's room, choosing the color is the fun part. Let your child guide your choice, but make sure to put forth some ideas of your own. A favorite piece of furniture, a rug, a bed cover, some special pillows, a poster—almost any decorative element can inspire and inform your choice. Just be sure your inspiration comes from an item that will be a favorite for some time to come (you'd hate to be back at square one within the calendar year). If your daughter has a beloved dollhouse, for example, one that's been passed between generations in your family, why not choose its color scheme for your daughter's real-life curtains and walls?

As with everything involving children, be sure to present your child with carefully selected options, ones that you, as a parent, can live with. The decision-making process may even be one that you, as a parent, can learn from. Who's to say that your son or daughter's adventurous color sense wouldn't spark your own imagination? You may be pleasantly surprised by his or her ability to create sophisticated and unusual color combinations that work.

When choosing color for a child's room, bear in mind that many adult choices don't apply. That putty color may look great in your office conference room, but it would seem downright drab in the room of a boy who loves orange and yellow. Conversely, the colors your children dream of—fuchsia, say, or lemon yellow—may not be something you can make peace with at home. In a case like this, compromise. If you hate a fluorescent shade of green favored by your offspring, why not suggest a paler version? Or you could place the child's longed-for color on one wall and use a complementary shade on the other three. Alternatively, you could simply use your child's favorite color for the sheets or curtains.

Some designers have creative ways of dealing with the unusual color requests that come their way. When interior designer Alexandra Stoddard's daughter was four, she requested a room that was entirely pink,

CLOCKWISE FROM TOP LEFT: An eclectic mix can work well if colors are repeated within each pattern.

Colorful tasseled tiebacks and blanket stitching add a homey touch to these simple felt curtains.

A plain wood box with compartments is transformed with playful use of color and the addition of mismatched wood pulls.

Bold graphics turn a nonskid floor mat into a great kids' room accent.

from ceiling to floor. Her mother thought not. She compromised by painting the floors pink, the walls white, and the ceiling blue. When the eight-year-old son of one of her clients begged for a room with lots of black, Stoddard came up with a design that would accommodate both this aspiring rebel and his more conservative parents. She created a black floor with glossy white walls, and she accented the room with black-and-white polka-dot window shades, and electric-yellow pillows.

Another interior designer, Agnes Bourne, recalls that a client's child also wanted a black room. Bourne gave it to him, but in a way that was far from gloomy: she had one wall painted in chalk-board paint, the others in bright white. A white wall can lighten any room, as it did in this boy's room. Painting most of the walls white allows the child to have the color of his or her choice, but in a way that's toned down and much easier to live with.

Exploring color with your child can be a fascinating experience. Try scattering paint chips across a table-top, and have him or her tell you what he or she sees in each shade. Examine elements from nature—seashells, vegetables, even the sky—and talk about what you see as you examine them. You may want to turn to favorite toys, even favorite foods, for inspiration. Point out the pleasing shade of red on a toy soldier's uniform or the delicious color of Granny

OPPOSITE, LEFT: You and your child can look to nature for color ideas.

OPPOSITE, RIGHT: Toys, supplies, and treasures can be stored in Color-by-Number Boxes.

ABOVE: A favorite toy can provide the inspiration for a color scheme. When in doubt, use splashes of color sparingly on single walls, trim, and borders.

Smith apples. Analyze a pigeon feather, noting the subtle variations of gray it contains. Chances are that by the end of one of these visual exploration sessions both you and your child will be seeing hues in new and different ways. Arriving at a color scheme you both like will become easier and easier as you talk.

Color is subtle. It changes constantly, depending on light and shadow, the hues that surround it, the surface it's used on. When choosing your palette, make sure to study the paint or fabric samples you're considering at different times of the day, and at night under lamplight. Because light colors look deeper under shadow, and because the room you're decorating is a bedroom (and therefore often used at night), it's a good idea to choose a color that's paler than the shade you first envisioned. A room's illumination, more than anything, sets its tone; incandescent light-bulbs give off a yellow cast that turns blue tones to gray but deepens oranges, yellows, and reds. Remember, too, that we identify color in part by the shades that surround it; so be sure to consider how a color will look against its neighboring hues and patterns.

You'll want to decide on the best color for the walls, ceiling, and floor first; then move on to the accent shades—the colors of draperies, shelves, toy chests, and other accessories. Whatever palette you do select, make sure to test it first. Paint a small section of the wall (or a piece of primed Masonite) with the color you're contemplating, before moving on to the rest of the room. Live with the color for a few days to make sure that it's right—for you and for your children.

story: **Julia's Room**

Julia and her parents wanted a warm pink-and-red palette—and lots of fantasy—for her room. Architects David Weingarten and Lucia Howard worked with these tones, combining them in inventive ways that related to the Spanish-style architecture of the family's home. In Julia's room "we chose motifs found in Spanish colonial architecture—squares related to the cross, the four-pointed star—blown way up," Weingarten says. Most dramatically, he and Howard transformed the child's ceiling into an ongoing light show, with thin wire tracks suspending an array of

fantastical features. Each night, before she goes to sleep, Julia gazes up at the pink-and-salmon-colored squares on her ceiling and sees her favorite colors. She delights in the silvery wires that crisscross the ceiling, from which tiny lights—shaped like dragonflies, flying octopuses, even eggs—are hung. Combined with silver spheres painted on the ceiling, these figures create a galaxy of mysterious, twinkling lights. (Since

OPPOSITE: In this cozy, colorful room, there's a play area and one in which to work. Combining unusual colors—such as the brilliant salmon, pink, lime, and burnt orange shades shown here—works fine, as long as they're anchored by a strong graphic and limited to one plane.

RIGHT: The ceiling—a collage of color—has a silver-colored square at its center. Tiny lights, in fanciful shapes, run on linear tracks that follow the graphics on the ceiling. When kept low, these lights, which are on dimmers, create a magical, starlike effect.

this particular galaxy is controlled by a dimmer switch, it can be soft at bedtime, and bright at other times.)

Julia's favorite colors are everywhere: her sheets are red, and there's a pink-and-yellow plaid quilt. Even her bedroom furniture, which includes a bookcase and a computer desk, is a deep, muted pink. The unusual cutout chair with a face on it may look like a child's piece, but it's actually sized for an adult and can be used for years to come. Toys are stored in rose-colored, stackable bins, pull-out drawers, and shallow, open shelves that surround the bed. "I like this best," Julia says, pointing to the bookcase that overflows with toys. But she's also enchanted by the show that takes place on her ceiling each night after lights-out. "One night she looked at the lights," her mother reports, "and said, 'This is magic.'"

ABOVE LEFT: The bright colors of this bedding and headboard unit echo the dramatic hues of the room's ceiling. The open shelves above the bed are perfect for displaying favorite stuffed animals and books.

LEFT: Smaller items and secret treasures can be stashed away in this headboard unit's raspberry- and purple-colored drawers.

RIGHT: This desk and chair are positioned to avoid window glare on the computer screen. They're also great examples of whimsical furniture pieces that work for both children and adults.

★ SURFACES

The surfaces in a child's room seem to matter more than those in rooms designed for adults. After all, how many grown-ups would even consider painting their bedroom ceiling magenta, coloring their closet door orange, or adding a circus-themed mural on one wall? Yet there's no holding back when there's a child involved. Walls and floors can be transformed in any number of ways, including stenciling, polishing, painting, even sandblasting. There's virtually no end to how you can transform your child's room.

The following sections take a step-by-step approach to each aspect of your child's room. And who knows? Perhaps by the end of the process, you may find yourself getting ideas for your own bedroom, too.

The dreamy images on this girl's room wall transform her small bedroom into a fantasy retreat.

WALLS AND CEILINGS

The design for any room must begin with its walls. Walls do more than enclose and shelter, they also set the scene. Once a room's color has been chosen, there are numerous paint treatments that can enhance it further. By stenciling, stamping, or glazing, for example, you can make the walls as special as the furniture. Consult how-to books, or your local paint or craft-supply store, for detailed instructions regarding any decorating techniques you decide to try.

Although walls are the obvious place for your child's favorite colors, don't neglect the ceiling. This is the last surface your child will see at the end of the day—why not make it conducive to wonderful dreams? We've already seen how Julia's ceiling came alive with unexpected elements, including magical, starlike lights. Other designs, even less-ambitious ones, can be equally effective. Consider adding simple glow-in-the-dark moon and star stickers. Try a mural—clouds on the ceiling are a classic. Or try an elaborate picture or pattern, perhaps one applied by a local artist. (Craft-supply stores can be a good source for the names of decorative artists.) And don't forget that any technique that works on a wall—from stenciling to stamping—will enhance a ceiling, too. The only difference, of course, is access. You may want to get your child's input on the ceiling design, but you should definitely adopt a no-kids-on-ladders rule, no matter who's doing the actual work. Regardless what your budget is, the walls and ceiling can be places for bold color and fantasy of all kinds.

Before you begin, remove loose paint and buildup with a putty knife. Repair cracks, holes, and uneven surfaces using Spackle or a similar compound. Use a caulking gun to fill in cracks and crevices. Prime surfaces as necessary before applying the first coat of paint. Keep in mind that some of the following techniques can disguise damage, too. Ragging and sponging, in particular, are good finishes to turn to if you want to camouflage an uneven or cracked finish.

SPATTERING is a decorative technique wherein two or three paint colors are flicked onto a wall. Make sure to carefully prepare the room before you use this technique, taping off or otherwise covering all surfaces that you don't want spattered. When you're ready, dip a brush in paint, then sharply hit the brush handle against a piece of wood held in the other

Safety Tip

Whenever you're using paint—particularly when children are present—you should work only in a well-ventilated area, using nontoxic, water-based paints.

hand, so that paint sprays in dots over the wall surface. Wait for one color to dry before applying the next. Although this procedure is fun—perhaps a little too fun for children, from an adult's point of view—you might not want to enlist young helpers, since it can also be fairly difficult to control.

STENCILING is an easy way to personalize a space and incorporate a favorite theme, from cats to space-ships, in a room. You can stencil a border on the wall near the ceiling, at chair-rail height, or, for that matter, almost anywhere else. And stenciling isn't just for the walls—it can be a great way to unify mismatched furniture or decorate the floor.

Children can easily create their own stencils by photocopying a strong, simple design such as a house, dog, or flower. Stencils can be a single image or a border of related images. Each photocopy should be traced with an indelible marker onto a piece of stiff Mylar (available from art-supply stores), then carefully cut out with an X-acto knife (parental help is imperative here!). Stencils can also be bought, of course; most of the ones sold at art- and craft-supply stores are made of plastic and are even easier to use than the cardboard kind. In addition, there are several Web sites where stencil patterns can be purchased.

If your child is old enough to stencil his or her own walls, you should first affix the stencil to the wall for him or her, using either painter's tape or stencil spray adhesive. This way, the child can paint—using water-based acrylic, latex, or stencil paint—without having to continually hold the template in place. Paint small sections at a time, taking care not to apply too much paint (otherwise, paint might bleed below the stencil). Allow the paint to dry before you remove the stencil from the wall or surface. When you reach the corner of a surface, try to end with the entire design. If this doesn't work, try stenciling in half of it, or however much fits. Wash your stencils periodically as you go, using warm water and soap. It's probably best to have several stencils on hand so that you and your child can be painting some while others are drying in place.

STAMPING, like stenciling, is another great way to add color and interest to walls. Some wonderful stamp patterns and motifs are available, ranging from palm trees to cowboy hats, which can be found at paint and hardware stores. Stamps also work beautifully on primed wood furniture and on accessories such as toy boxes. You and your child can even combine several stamps to create a frieze around the room, whether at the top of a wall or at chair-rail height. Stamps can be used with latex paint and applied to any primed wall with a matte surface (it's best to avoid using gloss and semi-gloss paints since they may cause stamps to slide during application). To use, roll out a thin layer of paint onto a smooth surface such as Plexiglas, press the stamp in, then remove excess paint by lightly stamping on scrap paper before applying to the wall. (Parental help is a necessity for children under seven, who may have trouble applying equal pressure to stamps, particularly on vertical surfaces.)

GLAZING, which involves mixing a glaze product with paint and applying many layers of color, in various intensities, is a more complex procedure. Glazing produces a deep, rich color, where multiple dark-, medium-, and light-colored coats of one hue are layered on a wall or other surface. Colors that are related but not identical, such as coral and pink, can also be layered together. When it's added to paint, the glazing medium causes the paint to dry at a slower rate. It's during this extended drying time that the surface can be played with—and when the magic takes place.

There are many glazing kits on the market; glazing elements can also be bought separately at many paint stores. There are numerous ways to work with glazing. One of the most popular is achieved by sponging the glaze onto a wall, freshly painted in a light, neutral color. After the base coat is dry, put on rubber gloves and use a sea sponge to apply a darker coat of paint that's been mixed with glazing medium. (Glazing tints can be combined. You may want to use a slightly darker tint of the color for the first coat, combined with another, different yet compatible, shade.) To build up color depth, additional coats can be applied after the first coat dries. For best results, you should work in small, manageable sections—2 by 3 feet is a good size. If you work in a larger area, the paint may dry too quickly and you won't be able to create an even finish.

Another method of glazing is to apply the glaze-paint mixture with a roller or paintbrush, then remove some of the paint by lightly dabbing it with crumpled cheesecloth, in order to create a subtle pattern on the paint surface. You may also use paper towels, making sure to replace each towel after it becomes saturated. As with all paint treatments, it's probably best to do a trial run by glazing a small part of a wall, letting it dry, and examining the results, before moving on to the entire room.

Another popular glazing technique, called ragging, is to lightly rub the wall with a glaze-dipped rag, for a light-and-dark effect that resembles marbling. By pressing soft, bunched-up rags (or even paper towels) into wet glaze and then against the wall, you can create all sorts of special effects. If the wall is ocher-colored, for example, you may want to rag over its surface with a paler shade of yellow, resulting in a subtle, parchment-like appearance. For more intensity, try ragging one bright color over another. Use lint-free rags, cheesecloth, or paper towels; make sure the

rags are bunched up so that the folds create a pattern in the glaze. Your results will be best when two people are working together, so this can be a great project to share with an older child. One person should apply glaze to the wall; the other should follow close behind, while the glaze is still wet, and rag the wall's surface.

STRIPES of alternating pastel colors—vertical stripes, in particular—can bring a bold yet understated sophistication to a child's room. Painting them is easy, but meticulous preparation work is required. First, measure the width of the wall you want to paint. Take this measurement and divide it until you find the best stripe width for the space; the wall will look best if it contains identically sized stripes. Using a level, carefully pencil in the stripes and tape off alternating stripes with painter's or masking tape, in order to ensure straight, even lines. Carefully paint the first color, filling in every other stripe, and then let the paint dry. Next, remove and reapply the tape, so that the stripes still to be painted are exposed, and carefully paint these in the contrasting shade.

WALLPAPER is another great way to decorate a child's room. Don't choose a design that depicts the cartoon fad of the week, though, since stripping off old paper and adding new wallpaper is a chore. Great wallpapers can be found at specialty shops and paint stores, as can books and other instructional materials that explain how to hang them. Wallpapers come in two varieties—prepasted and regular. Although the

ABOVE: A border at chair-rail height (scaled lower for kids) is a simple way to add a personal and sophisticated touch.

BELOW: Vintage wall papers—and some excellent reproductions—are charming and can be found at select antique stores (see "Resources," page 150).

former is easier, choosing regular wallpaper will offer you a wider choice of patterns and styles.

If wallpapering seems like too much trouble, opt for a wallpaper border instead, affixing it to the wall at cornice height, where the ceiling meets the wall, so it acts as a frieze around the perimeter of the room. (Although it's certainly permissible to hang the border at a lower height, hanging it at ceiling height is certainly the easiest way to keep it straight and completely visible.) Borders, which typically measure about 6 inches in height, are meant to complement matching wallpaper, but they can also look just fine when hung on a painted wall instead. Available in the same patterns and themes—from cartoon characters to football teams—as wallpaper, they liven up a room with a minimum of effort.

Another alternative is to use only selected elements of a favorite paper on the walls, without covering them entirely. Choose a wallpaper that contains a bold or outsize image, then just cut out the figures you want to use, and affix them to the wall with wallpaper paste. Obviously, you'll want to choose designs that are compatible with the paint on the walls.

CHALKBOARD PAINT Another wall treatment with appeal for children is chalkboard paint, which comes in black and green shades. This paint is exactly what you might expect—a dense, opaque liquid that can be used as a chalkboard after it dries. Although I wouldn't recommend covering an entire room with this paint, I'd definitely designate at least one section of a wall—at a kid-friendly height, of course—as a zone for temporary works of art. Bear in mind that chalk makes dust, which is the enemy of dark carpets, not to mention the allergies it can cause. An easier, and perhaps less troublesome, alternative is a magnetic white board, which could be turned into a fun, constantly changing exhibition space. Another option is to affix a large sketch pad to a wall and keep assorted paints and colored pencils nearby for easy access.

story: A Hilltop Playroom

Architects Richard Fernau and Laura Hartman know that children love to draw. So when they were asked to design a bedroom for a country-dwelling four-year-old boy, they added a child-height chalkboard around its entire perimeter with a metal chalkboard-rail at the top and a wooden strip at the bottom, to collect chalk dust.

The house is wedge shaped, and the boy's corner room is sited deep in the side of a grassy hill. Each morning when he wakes up, he can look directly out at the grasses that grow up to window height—just as if he'd woken up from a nap in a meadow, on a lazy summer's afternoon.

OPPOSITE: This metal chalkboard-rail is the standard schoolroom type. A simple wood ledge could also be used.

ABOVE: In this little boy's room nestled into a California hillside, a real chalkboard wraps around the perimeter below chair-rail height.

FLOORS

Nothing compares with wood. Wooden floors warm a room with their tawny shades, and they're endlessly versatile in appearance, seeming brighter or darker, depending on their surroundings. They're easy to clean and can last a lifetime, even longer. A wooden floor in poor shape can easily be renewed, by sanding and adding a coat of urethane or by finishing it with deck paint in almost any color.

TONGUE AND GROOVE, durable and easy to finish, is the most commonly used kind of wood floor. The traditional way to treat these floors is to sand them, then stain them. There's a whole spectrum of stains to choose from. A cherry stain will bring out the floor's red and auburn shades; oak will bring out its rich brown tones. For a wonderful, pale effect, try scrubbing a sanded wood floor with a ready-made bleach solution, then sealing it with acrylic or water-borne urethane. There is a two-part solution specially made for bleaching wood floors— the two parts of the bleaching solution are mixed together and applied to the floor according to manufacturer's directions. A basic white stain can also be applied to the floor. Both options are available at high-quality paint stores. Floors can also be professionally "pickled"—a multiple-step procedure involving sanding, bleaching, and several layers of applied color and sealer.

PARQUETRY is a centuries-old method of flooring or paneling in which wood is cut into geometric patterns and laid or inlaid into the floor. You should maintain a parquet floor as you would a tongue-and-groove floor, with occasional waxing or polishing, and perhaps refinishing after it becomes worn. It would be a shame to cover the geometric designs of parquetry with paint. If you do want to add more pattern to a parquet floor, why not create a subtle checkerboard pattern, in which alternating parquet squares are stained in a paler shade than the other, darker squares? In this way, you can add emphasis to the floor, while allowing the beauty of the parquetry to show through.

SYNTHETIC WOOD FLOORING, which is typically made from polyurethane, makes a wonderful floor for a child's room. It's tough, durable, and almost impossible to mar. Synthetic wood floors, like natural wood, come in a tongue-and-groove construction and are relatively easy to install. They need no polishing, waxing, or other kind of treatment. A popular brand is Pergo, a Swedish product now in use around the world.

Wood floors may be decorated by using stencils, trompe l'oeil, or coats of paint. Although painting a floor is relatively easy, the process can be time consuming—it can take days for all the layers to dry.

Because kids, especially young ones, spend so much time playing on the floor, careful consideration should be given to selecting the right material.

For this reason, it's important to pick a color or design for your child's floor that will appeal to both of you for years to come.

When preparing a floor for painting or other treatments, including stenciling, make sure the wood is smooth and that any holes in it have been filled in with putty. Sand the floor, preferably with a commercial sander. Sanding a wood floor should be an adults-only project. The process creates an enormous amount of dust, which is dangerous to the lungs if inhaled. Make sure there's plenty of ventilation, and wear a protective mask over your nose and mouth while you're working. After sanding, sweep and mop the floor several times before setting to work.

Thanks to numerous books and crafts kits, many sophisticated decorating techniques are now available to everyone. Faux finishes—in which gesso, gilt, and other materials are used to create the look of marble, ivory, even lapis lazuli, on wood—have been around for centuries. While many of these finishes may seem too formal for a child's room, there are plenty of variations that are not, including fun trompe l'oeil effects. A good painter or muralist can take things even further, creating exciting murals on floors, as well as walls. What floor wouldn't come to life with the addition of, say, a view of a tiger in its cage, as seen from above, or a mini-ballpark, complete with painted bases and a pitcher's mound?

STENCILING is a wonderful way to decorate a floor. It offers you the versatility of carpeting, with much less expense, and it adds interest to even the most understated space. Now, with the widespread availability of plastic stencils (sold at craft- and art-supply stores), the process has become easier than ever.

FLOOR TILES made of vinyl, also known as PVC (polyvinyl chloride), now come in a wider range of designs and hues than ever before, due to recent manufacturing developments. Vinyl floors are also easy to clean and are impervious to children's spills. Like linoleum, these tiles are fairly easy to install. Note that installing vinyl tiles is one project that should not be shared with kids since it involves the use of both sharp instruments and toxic-smelling tape or glue.

Vinyl tiles can easily be transformed into yet another decorative surface in your child's room. You can create colorful patterns by cutting the tiles into various shapes and reassembling them. Try cutting them on the diagonal and then, using two or more tile colors, make a pattern of colored triangles, or any other playful shape. Again, while you may want to consult with your children about their preferred colors and patterns, the actual cutting should be done by adults.

RUBBER FLOORING, made from by-products of the petrochemical industry, is another bedroom or playroom option. It comes in sheets and tiles and is as easy to maintain as vinyl and linoleum. Plus, it has the added advantages of absorbing noise, being warmer to the touch, and being more durable than vinyl or

TOOLS

- pencil
- foam or bristle brushes, in
  ½-inch or 1-inch widths
- paint tray
- paint roller
- roller covers

MATERIALS

- precut stencils (available
  at paint and craft-supply
  stores) in a diamond design
- spray adhesive or drafting
  tape (available at hardware,
  paint, and craft-supply stores)
- water-based acrylic, latex, or
  stencil paint in two bright,
  contrasting colors (yellow
  and red, or blue and purple,
  for example)
- paper towels
- nonyellowing polyurethane
  sealant

project: **Harlequin Floor**

1 Prepare your wood floor as described on page 32.

2 Measure and mark out the design on the floor in pencil, so that the pattern will be evenly spaced and uniform in appearance.

3 Beginning with the area of the room that's farthest from the door, apply the stencil to the floor using the spray adhesive, according to the markings you made in step two. Pour a small amount of paint into a jar or bowl, then dip your brush into it and wipe the brush with a paper towel to remove excess paint. Now, start painting! Be careful not to use too much paint, in order to prevent it from running or smearing. Wash the stencil periodically as you work.

4 When you finish painting each section, move the stencil over and begin again. If you work carefully, you won't need to wait for the paint to dry between sections. When you come to a corner, try to end with a complete design. If this isn't possible, you may have to paint in some of it by hand.

5 After you finish stenciling, let the paint dry for a day before sealing the floor with polyurethane varnish, using the paint tray, roller, and roller covers. Although one coat will do, applying two is advised for high-traffic areas.

linoleum. Installation is relatively easy. Rubber floors typically come with raised round or square surface patterns and are often used in commercial kitchens, ice rinks, and playgrounds. They are designed to provide excellent grip underfoot, helping to keep even the most energetic child from slipping, so they're also relatively safe. The one disadvantage of rubber floors is that there is a relatively limited selection of patterns to choose from. Still, they come in bright colors and have their own high-tech feel.

The big news about linoleum is that it's not dreary anymore. It now comes in a wide range of colors and patterns, many of which will appeal to kids. Available in both sheets and precut tiles, linoleum is relatively easy to install. Check the manufacturer's information for step-by-step installation instructions.

CORK FLOORING comes from the bark of the cork oak tree, which grows mainly in the western Mediterranean regions. Cork is harvested about once a decade from these trees, which go on to grow a whole new layer. Cork is a wonderful material for floors. Besides being tough, with good sound-insulating properties, it's also flexible, slip-resistant, and comfortable beneath the feet. This is a great surface for kids, almost as resilient as linoleum, but somewhat cozier. Cork is sold in various shades and several finishes, including sanded, waxed, and vinyl-coated. For ease of cleaning, vinyl-coated cork is superior, requiring only a mild soap-and-water solution to keep it maintained. The standard 12-by-12-inch

tiles need to be glued to a smooth surface with tile adhesive. For a checkerboard effect, alternate shades—or try your own design. Because cork floors absorb noise, they work wonders in rooms inhabited by high-decibel children.

RUGS

When it comes to floor coverings, nothing beats a nice, soft rug or carpet for warming up a room. Any bedroom becomes instantly cozy when there's a rug on the floor. However, though a rug makes a warm—and warmly colored—addition to a sleeping area, you should probably consider a more durable, stain-resistant surface, such as rubber or linoleum, for areas devoted to play. If there's already a good-quality carpet on the floor, you might want to consider covering it with something pretty but less expensive, until the messier years of childhood have passed. Colorful kilim and dhurrie rugs are two wonderfully inexpensive solutions; tatami mats are another. (Remember that for all smaller carpets and mats, nonslip rug pads are a must for underneath.) However they're used, floor coverings can define a room. Those discussed following are natural choices for kids' rooms.

This distinctive multicolored linoleum "carpet" protects the wall-to-wall carpeting beneath it.

AREA RUGS can do wonders to brighten and personalize a room. These can be placed on almost any floor surface and in almost any configuration. When placing rugs, remember that symmetrical isn't always best; sometimes a rug placed diagonally looks great, too. And, unlike fitted carpeting, area rugs don't just have to be synthetic or wool. There are wonderful ones available in such materials as cotton, silk, chenille, and other fabrics. Whatever area rugs you choose for your child's room, be sure to use a nonslip underlay, or rug pad, beneath it, not just to prevent it from slipping, but also to minimize abrasion and ensure a longer life for the carpet. The best rug pads come in rubber or sponge, but they're also available in felt.

Machine-made kilims and flatweave rugs are produced throughout the world, in countries such as Mexico, India, Pakistan, and Turkey. Flatweave rugs are thinner than their knotted woolen counterparts; they feature bright colors and geometric patterns, and some have figures and floral patterns. Typically inexpensive, they can be a wonderful addition to any child's room. Inexpensive Mexican flatweave carpets, often woven in neon-bright colors, are plentiful in the United States and can be found at many ethnic shops and stores selling home accessories. Add layer upon layer of these or other flatweaves on the floor for a comfortable, multicolored look. Other fun floor coverings include rugs that are embroidered, crocheted, or braided. Although many of the braided rugs available today are expensive antiques (the results of a traditional early-American handicraft),

cheaper reproductions can also be found in various stores and catalogs.

For millennia, natural fibers have been harvested and made into mats for indoor use. Sisal, which is formed from the leaves of agave plants, is a particularly popular alternative to carpeting and other coverings. Other popular fibers for matting include rush, jute, abaca, and grass. Sisal comes in various weaves, including a herringbone pattern, and a sisal-wool mix, which looks like tweed and is available in various colors. Sisal and other natural-fiber floor coverings are available in fitted and area-rug styles. Parents should be warned, though, that, as beautiful as sisal is, it tends to absorb spills and can be difficult to clean. For this reason, a dark color is probably the best choice for children's rooms.

FITTED, or WALL-TO-WALL, carpeting is one of the least expensive options when it comes to floor covering. Fitted, machine-made carpets come in three styles: woven, tufted, and bonded. They also are made with many materials, including wool, nylon, polyester, acrylic, and polypropylene. Nothing beats wool for coziness, but it's also the most expensive carpeting material. Typically, the price drops as the wool content goes down and the proportion of synthetics goes up. Where budgets allow, a mix of eighty percent wool to twenty percent nylon is probably ideal: the synthetic fibers help the carpet last longer, while the high proportion of wool makes for a more pleasing appearance. When choosing carpeting for a child's room, you may want to opt for a higher percentage of synthetic material, since it has superior stain resistance.

Most manufacturers use an eight-point grading system to rate carpeting and area rugs, labeling them as light duty, medium duty, heavy duty, or extra heavy duty. In general, darker, patterned carpets will keep their original appearance longer than will lighter-colored ones. Don't try to install wall-to-wall carpeting on your own! This is a complex and tedious process that's best left to professionals. And it's absolutely not an appropriate task for children.

CARPET TILES in wool or nylon are decorative and practical, since they can be replaced individually in areas of excess wear. They usually measure 20 by 20 inches and come in great colors, from scarlet to lavender. These tiles can be easily cut, then combined together in interesting ways. You could even try putting them together in a checkerboard pattern, using two contrasting colors. Like other kinds of carpets, carpet tiles are available in woven, tufted, and bonded styles. Because they are thick, they don't need to be placed over padding, glued, or taped down, except in areas of heavy traffic, such as at the tops and bottoms of stairs.

A **FLOOR CLOTH** is a fun, and far less expensive, alternative to carpeting. Made of sturdy canvas and coated with paint, floor cloths cover the floor and are a great way to introduce a color scheme or pattern into a room. Many decorative artists—the same people you might hire to do a mural—are happy to work on floor cloths. But you should also consider allowing your child to paint his or her own floor covering—you might even be able to join him or her in a day of painting. Just be sure to choose a heavy-weight canvas and, after the paint has dried, to seal it into the cloth with polyurethane (making sure there's plenty of ventilation, and no kids present, when you do so). If there's a downside to floor cloths, it's the lack of comfort—being pile-free, they don't have the deep, soft coziness of a carpet.

Safety Tip

For health reasons, when painting floors, be sure to use water-based urethane, as opposed to polyurethane, a synthetic varnish. Because the toxins in polyurethane remain in the room for an unknown period of time even after the substance dries, it's best to avoid using it in a child's room. Urethane is also less apt to yellow over time than its synthetic cousin. Check labels carefully, though—the terms polyurethane and urethane are sometimes used interchangeably. No matter what it's called, be sure that the varnish you take home is water based.

LIGHT

Light defines our days and nights. Our first experience of the day, even before we open our eyes, is our perception of the sunlight in the room. Our last vision before sleep may be of the glow cast by a street lamp as it filters through the blinds, or of a comforting strip of illumination shining in under the bedroom door. Even small children are aware that the sun is bright and high at midday, low and golden toward evening, and, at sunset, variously pink, red, and purple. The day's progression of light is something children know instinctively.

Night is a powerful time for children, in all sorts of ways. While it's a time when their fears may awaken, it's also a time when many kids half expect their toys and other beloved objects to come to life. The experience of light lasts all through the night. For kids, the time when the moonlight beams into their bedrooms and the stars first appear, twinkling like Christmas lights and beckoning to be wished upon, is pure magic. When lighting is used inventively, this same enchantment can be there for the asking, every night of the week.

OPPOSITE: There's nothing like the cheery warmth of sunlight to brighten a child's room.

FOLLOWING PAGE: A small playroom benefits from two generous windows on the back wall. The abundance of natural light makes the space more cheerful and open.

project: **Lacy Lamp**

In this project, frilly doilies are used as stencils for adding an intricate pattern to a lamp shade.

❶ Hold the doilies against the lamp shade to find the arrangement that pleases you most—you can overlap them for a scalloped effect, or position them several inches apart. You can also try cutting the doilies to create new patterns and shapes.

❷ Spray adhesive and attach tiny bits of transparent tape onto the backs of the doilies and fix them to the lamp shade, making sure that the doilies are firmly tacked down at edges and corners. Be sure to position the transparent tape carefully so that it doesn't cover or block any of the holes in the doilies.

❸ Spray paint onto the shade, taking care to spray the holes in the doilies evenly and completely. Remove the doilies just after painting, before the adhesive has time to dry.

★ LIGHTING

When evaluating your child's lighting requirements, keep in mind the need for a strong ceiling light, for overall illumination, as well as task lights for reading and other focused activities. Some of these come in clip-on or gooseneck styles, perfect to clip to a

CLOCKWISE FROM LEFT: This inspired lampshade—half flowerpot, half hat—is just the kind of fun accessory that has enduring kid appeal. Don't hesitate to sprinkle humorous touches liberally around children's rooms—they really appreciate them!

This lantern fixture, while designed for outdoor use, brings a nice touch of whimsy to a child's room. It's also an effective way to keep small hands away from hot lightbulbs.

Although this ceramic lamp, complete with elaborately pleated shade, is sophisticated, it still has that certain magic that appeals to a child.

headboard for bedtime reading, or to place on a desk for doing homework. A source of soft, ambient lighting is also a plus, brightening the space and creating a cozy, fun atmosphere. There are numerous whimsical ambient lights available for children, from lamps with moon- and star-shaped shades, to strings of novelty lights—colored plastic fish, say, or bright-red jalapeño peppers. Night-lights can also add character to a child's room, with seemingly endless possibilities available, from rotating shadow theaters to simple, glowing, green rectangles.

Our eyes become more tired when the contrast between dark and light areas is strong, experts say. Overhead lights help create even illumination and cut the shadows. Dimmers can be added, for greater versatility. Although many standard, traditional overhead lamps are downright boring, there's no reason

the elements

43

why they need to be. Check out any lamp or hardware store to see how stylish the new designs are. Overhead lamps, while essential for general illumination, don't provide enough light for close work, such as reading, writing, or sewing. For these jobs, task lights are essential for reducing eyestrain and improving concentration.

When selecting task lights, choose child-friendly fixtures. "It should be something that they [children] can adjust," explains architect Lucia Howard, "but you want to keep their hands away from the bulb." Children's task lights should be easy to turn on and off and have sturdy, weighted bases. Some of the simplest and sleekest task lights—such as gooseneck lamps or classic industrial desk lamps—have adjustable or flexible arms. Make sure that desk lamps are placed at an angle so that they don't create glare on a computer screen. If your child likes to read in bed, see that his or her bedside lamp is positioned so that the light streams down from above, resulting in a soft, even illumination.

Lighting accessories such as switch plates and lamp shades don't need to be plain—they can be used to add an extra dose of fun to your overall design. Switch plates can be decorated in an infinite number of ways. You can make a colorful fingerprint design using water-based paint, for example, or you can use markers to create funky designs. (One easy way to foster a child's independence is to have the switch plates in his or her room moved down so that they're within reach.)

Lamp shades and bases offer another opportunity to bring whimsy and fantasy into a room. Paper shades can be painted, stamped, or stenciled, and quirky old lamp bases—found at garage sales and flea markets—can easily be refinished and given new life.

✋ Safety Tips

Avoid using halogen lamps in children's rooms. Used as reading light sources, they create too much contrast, and the extreme heat generated by their bulbs can be a serious fire hazard.

Keep all lights, even night-lights, away from flammable materials, including bedding, curtains, and paper products. For extra safety, substitute a miniature fluorescent bulb for the four- or seven-watt bulb in your child's night-light.

Always have old lamp bases professionally rewired, as needed. This inexpensive precaution is absolutely necessary when the lamp is to be used in a child's room.

All lamps used in kids' rooms should bear the UL seal, which indicates that they've been tested and proven to be safe. Also, check labels to find out the maximum safe wattage—on many small lamps it's 60 watts or fewer.

ABOVE LEFT: As this vintage light fixture, with its bold colors and dangling bells, demonstrates, fun lighting doesn't have to be new.

ABOVE RIGHT: With its tiny, smiling face, this bold lamp base—a flea-market find—truly lights up a room.

Rickrack Light

Although the light fixture shown in this photo was bought ready made from Goodnight Rooms, this festive night-light can be created using a store-bought sconce shade. Decorate it with rick-rack, stencils, or stamps in a favorite theme.

★ WINDOW TREATMENTS

Children have their own particular sensitivities to light. One child I know dislikes having an indoor light on when there is natural light in the room—she claims to find the mix of the two kinds of lights disturbing. Other kids feel most secure under the cheerful glow of bright overhead lights, at all times of the day. Any discussion regarding window treatments must begin with the needs of your child. For a child who's frightened of the dark, for example, the most comforting window solution might be pale curtains that hide scary black windows. A child who has trouble sleeping

This simple felt curtain has blanket stitching and a tassel tieback. An extra tassel used as a pull for the blackout shade adds a playful touch and coordinates the look. (See "Blanket Stitched Felt Curtain," page 55.)

may be happiest with an extra-dark window covering.

The immediate environment will also dictate choices. For a ground-floor bedroom, a venetian-style blind, one that allows in light but obscures the view into the room, may be best. Or, if you live in an older house where windows are drafty, you might want to choose translucent honeycomb shades, which have strong insulating properties.

The following are the most commonly used window treatments—one of them is sure to be right for your child's room.

HONEYCOMB SHADES look just like pleated shades from the front. But seen from the side, they reveal their honeycomb-like construction; the cell structures act as a heat insulator, keeping heat from passing through. They're great for blocking drafty windows, making chronically chilly bedrooms seem cozy and warm. They come in several different varieties, and are categorized according to their ability to insulate. These shades are frequently made of silk or other soft fabrics (even blackout fabric) and are available in a whole wardrobe of colors. They're beautiful when extended but are so compact as to be invisible when pulled shut.

STANDARD ROLLER SHADES are an easy way to introduce color and texture into a room. Once made only in plain white, they're now available in a wide range of colors and styles in fabric and paper. Even shade pulls now come in many styles, from frosted colored beads to silky tassels. Their appearance may have changed, but roller shades still work the way they always have. You tug the shade gently down to close it; when you want to open it again, you pull gently on it until it springs back up into place. Some children may have trouble operating spring-loaded pull shades, so it's important to avoid using poorer-quality ones, which may easily spring loose, in their rooms.

ROMAN SHADES, instead of rolling up, gather softly as you pull their cords. They come in numerous materials, from bamboo and other natural materials to linens and other fabrics. There's the casual type of Roman shade, one that has an inverted pleat at the top. There are flat Roman shades, which fold up at 6-inch intervals. Soft Roman shades feature overlapping folds, spaced at 4- to 6-inch intervals. Even the basic

Roman shade style can be bought with a difference—in a top-down version, rather than a bottom-up one.

Almost any store, catalog, or Web site that carries window shades should be able to make custom shades or blinds in a favorite fabric or hard-to-get color. An interior designer might also be a good source for custom window treatments.

VENETIAN BLINDS are sleek and colorful and don't look a bit like their more awkward-looking ancestors. But the principle behind them—horizontal slats that can be opened or closed by degrees—remains the same. Venetian blinds can be purchased in either metal or wood and in numerous sizes, with slats that measure from $\frac{1}{2}$ inch to 3 inches wide. They can also be found in a rainbow of child-appealing colors.

WOOD BLINDS have 1- to 3-inch-wide horizontal slats and are available in a variety of finishes and colors. Even the twill tape that connects the slats can make a bright statement, since it comes in many fabric styles and colors.

PLEATED SHADES come in many colors and materials, including crushed silk. Like blinds and honeycomb shades, they operate with a cord for raising and lowering. Because pleated shades tend to be more translucent than the pull-down variety, they may not be the best choice for children of napping age, who might have trouble falling asleep in bright

CLOCKWISE FROM ABOVE: Simple white curtains are made more interesting with the addition of an oversized checkered pattern for borders and ribbon ties.

This simple but elegant flat fabric panel was created by combining an understated classic animal print with broad strips of linen in a compatible neutral tone.

Hooks and grommets are an easy and secure way to attach fabric panels to window frames.

Safety Tips

Keep window-blind cords away from small children at all times. Cords should be safely wrapped around a cleat near the top of the window and out of children's reach. Never place a crib near a window where a cord is hung, even one that's usually secured in a cleat. Adults should always open and close the blinds for smaller children.

Safety locks must be placed on all windows in homes with small children, in order to prevent kids from falling or climbing out. Secure locks so that the window can't be opened more than 3 inches.

The type of roller shade that is operated by a loop-and-pulley system that hangs at its side is easier for small children to use than is the traditional style of roller shade. Even so, the loops present a safety hazard for young kids and shouldn't be installed in their rooms.

Made in the Shade

You can transform virtually any fabric, including sheets, into shades. Store-bought blackout shades tend to get dirty quickly and don't add much character to a kid's room. There is a way to create customized shades using inexpensive fabric or sheets.

Home centers, some hardware stores, and specialty paint stores will laminate your fabric with opaque material and create standard roller shades. An oversized button attached with glue is a fun alternative to an old-fashioned pull.

daylight. And parents should note that pleated shades, while beautiful, can be relatively delicate; because of this, they may not be the most practical choice for a young child's room. (The paper variety, in particular, is unsuitable for a child's room.) In addition, light-colored pleated shades can be very difficult to clean.

CURTAINS do more than just shut out the light. They can also introduce pattern and color, from pastel sheers, to panels with grommets, to luxurious velvet drapes. While you may aim for subtlety in draperies for formal, more adult rooms, there's no reason to do so for kids. Curtains set the scene almost as effectively as paint color does, and there's no reason not to make them festive and fun.

You'll want to make sure that your child's draperies are kid friendly in terms of safety as well as appearance. Here, as everywhere in a kid's room, safety should rule. Invest in high-quality hardware and secure it well. See that curtain rings slide easily along the rod. And, once they're hung, test all curtains to make sure that opening and closing them requires only a gentle motion—tugging and yanking could lead to disastrous results. Floor-length drapes are probably not the best choice for a baby's room, since crawlers and toddlers can be counted on to use these for pulling themselves up to a standing position.

TAB-TOP curtains, which have loops of fabric that are sewn onto the tops, are probably the simplest

option available. Canvas tab-top panels can be purchased at fabric and specialty stores and in catalogs in wonderfully rich shades, such as eggplant and French blue. And they're remarkably easy to install. Just hang a rod—making sure it's secure—and loop the curtains through it. Tab-top curtains are less formal, less fussy, and far less expensive than traditional draperies. They're also safe, since no cords or pulleys are used. Their sole disadvantage is that they can be difficult for small children to open and close.

With **CLASSIC DRAPERIES**, it's all in the fold. Some gather into crescent-shaped loops. Others fall into neat pleats. And there are many other variations. When it comes to curtains, it's probably best to enlist the help of a decorator, a specialty shop staff member, or a fabric store employee in negotiating the seemingly endless array of choices. Your child's needs, of course, matter, too. For a light sleeper, make sure draperies are lined. If your son or daughter is afraid of the dark, you may want to choose material that allows for privacy but lets the moonlight shine through.

FABRIC VALANCES drape across the top of windows for a purely decorative effect. Soft, flowing, scalloped designs and tailored styles are among the choices available. Secure the fabric with curtain rods or special valance brackets, available at hardware stores. Valances also come in wooden versions, called cornices; some of these are covered in fabric and can be custom made using a favorite material from your child's room.

SWAGS—long, flowing pieces of fabric—are draped over the top of a window for decorative effect. Sometimes called scarves, they also serve to conceal curtain hardware. Decorative hooks are placed at the top of a window, on either side, so that the swags can be elegantly draped through them. Swag hooks can be made from lots of different objects, even decorative drawer pulls, offering yet another way to continue a theme or match other furniture.

CURTAIN RODS can be found in myriad designs, in both metal and wood. Add tiebacks if you want to secure curtains when they're open. Fun, decorative finials can punctuate the ends of curtain rods; and some are sold with matching tiebacks, in painted ceramic styles and carved animal shapes in wood.

TOP: Valances are an inventive way to conceal curtain hardware. Here, a velvet-clad valance is artfully matched with a pair of sheer polka-dot curtains.

BOTTOM: Wooden curtain rings and rods are easy for a child to use—look for hooks with clips if curtains will be laundered regularly.

story: **Nikki's Room**

Four-year-old Nikki liked bright hues—neon bright. Her parents hired Jill Wood and Gretchen Gibson, partners in an interior design company called A Child's Eye View (see "Resources," page 150), to revamp their daughter's room. By adding a few simple elements, the designers brought coherence to the room.

Could any interior space possibly be brighter than Nikki's room? Not very easily. It began with a hand-stitched red, blue, and yellow comforter. "The family

has a lot of African and South American ethnic art," said Wood, "so we wanted to keep that feeling of handmade pieces." They played off the comforter's primary-color palette by designing bright red-and-yellow felt curtains to match. Blanket stitching around the curtain edges, in contrasting chenille yarn, continues the handmade motif. Beneath the draperies, the designers dressed up ordinary pull shades by adding a tassel of the same chenille yarn.

project: **Blanket-Stitched Felt Curtain**

❶ Using chenille yarn and an embroidery needle, blanket-stitch around each edge of the felt (use two colors if you want to use different colors on different sides of the curtain). To create this traditional stitch, thread the chenille yarn through the needle and pull the yarn through the felt from back to front, making a loose stitch approximately ½ inch in from the edge. Then pass the needle through the loop and gently pull it taut, being careful that the fabric doesn't buckle when you do so. Stitches should be placed at ½-inch intervals.

❷ With heavy-duty thread, sew the wooden rings to the top of the curtain at a distance of about 4 inches apart.

❸ To make a tieback, tie the fifteen strands of chenille yarn together into a knot at one end, and then braid or twist them, separating by color if desired. Finish the braid by tying a knot 8 inches from the end, then trim the strands so that the ends are even. Stitch the center of the tieback to the outside edge of the curtain or attach it to a hook screwed into the window frame.

❹ To create a decorative tassel, use the ball of chenille yarn and unwind it a bit. Cut a 24-inch length, and set it aside. Take the yarn ball and wrap the yarn around the cardboard square one hundred times. Slide one of the 12-inch pieces of yarn in between the cardboard and the first bunch of yarn at the cardboard's midpoint. Tie this piece of yarn around the bunch of yarn, drawing it together. Slide the loop of yarn off the cardboard. Holding the loop by the ends of the tie, so that the bunched yarn hangs down, take the 24-inch length and wrap it tightly, at about 1 inch below the securing tie, around the doubled bunch six times. This will create the top knot of the tassel. Using sharp scissors, snip the long end of the loop so that the ends are even and the length you want. Hang the tassel from either end of the curtain rod with the remaining 12-inch piece of yarn. Make as many of these tassels, in as many colors, as you like, and hang them from the ends of the curtain rod with additional 12-inch pieces of yarn.

TOOLS
- embroidery needle
- fabric scissors

MATERIALS
- balls of chenille yarn in colors that contrast with the felt color
- 54-inch-wide piece of felt in the color of your choosing (use this fabric measurement for a 27-inch-wide window; for a window with a different width, use fabric that is twice the width of the window), cut to 2 inches longer the length of the window from top to bottom
- twelve wooden curtain rings (more for wider curtains)
- fifteen 36-inch lengths of chenille yarn, in three contrasting or coordinating colors
- ball of chenille yarn for tassel
- two 12-inch lengths of chenille yarn in a color that contrasts or coordinates with the color of the ball of yarn
- 6-by-6-inch piece of cardboard
- curtain rod

FURNITURE

"Keep it flexible!" architect Larry Bogdanow advises, when asked how to best furnish a child's room. Stores are full of imaginative pieces of furniture for kids, from chairs shaped like cartoon characters to tables that double as castles. Such pieces, though amusing at first, may lose their novelty as your child's interests change. (If you have several children, the appeal of these furnishings will, of course, be of longer duration.) Simple furniture designed for small adults will be practical for a much longer period than furniture designed for children. Almost any piece, too, can be made temporarily child-appropriate. You can add cartoon-themed fabric, for example, or a bright coat of paint; years later, you can rejuvenate the same piece of furniture by adding new upholstery or by stripping the finish back to its original tone.

If you do decide to buy children's furniture, look for pieces that can be adjusted and transformed as your child grows. Look for pieces that can accommodate changing interests. A chest that makes perfect storage for dolls, for example, should be able to accommodate CDs, basketballs, or craft supplies when your daughter is older. Think carefully before you buy and, if you include your child in the decision-making process, make sure to follow that time-honored rule of parenting—offer only choices you can live with. And, as with any purchase for a child, keep common-sense safety rules in mind.

This vintage bed features a delicately curved iron frame. Mixing older furniture—or hand-me-downs—with newer furniture can create an inviting and homey feel in a child's room.

★ BEDS

There are endless possibilities when it comes to choosing a child's bed. If you have a daughter who loves frills and feminine touches, why not buy a four-poster or sleigh bed (both of which are styles that will last all though the teenage years)? If space is an issue, a loft bed—which can accommodate a desk or play area underneath—might be ideal. For a child who has many sleepovers—or siblings—consider buying bunk beds or a trundle bed. A captain's bed, with drawer space underneath, can provide much-needed extra toy storage. Beds should be sturdy, above all; for this reason, hardwood or metal is best.

Acquiring a bed doesn't necessarily mean buying a new one. Any bed, when painted or stenciled, can be perfect for a child. Even a family antique, of nonstandard width, can always be resized. (Be sure, though, if an old bed has lead paint on it, that you have it stripped off before a new coat of paint is applied.)

Wooden beds, in particular, are wonderfully versatile. Headboards can be carved into shapes or made to look like wainscoting. And if your child loves fuchsia or chartreuse and begs for a bed in one of these bright colors, you can relax in the knowledge that this same piece of furniture can be repainted or

CLOCKWISE FROM TOP LEFT: An updated version of a canopy bed with a scalloped border sets the tone in this colorful room.

This sturdy bed, painted in rich blue, has a star cut into its headboard to let the sunlight or moonlight shine through.

An old-fashioned four-poster bed is charming and will never need replacing.

This cottage-style bed, in a lovely muted color, was a perfect flea-market find for this girl's room.

Safety Tips

No matter how old your child is, be sure to buy a guard rail for the top bunk of a bunk bed set, even if your child protests that such a thing is too babyish. Any sleepers can roll out of bed, even adults, and the results—particularly when there are toys scattered on the floor below—could be disastrous.

If your child suffers from asthma, be sure to determine the mattress's fill material, in order to make sure it won't cause an allergic reaction. For a highly allergic child, special plastic mattress covers can be used to reduce the numbers of dust mites.

stripped back down to the wood, if and when she tires of the hue.

A crucial consideration in a child's room is space for friends—sleepovers are, after all, almost every child's favorite kind of play date. Twin beds are perfect, if space permits; a trundle bed may be a good alternative if space is limited. A futon couch, preferably one in a bright, cheery pattern, can be used as a sofa, then unfolded for use as a mattress for sleepovers. Another easy solution is an inflatable mattress; many of these have built-in electric pumps for easy inflation and can be easily stored in a closet or under a bed. And, of course, bunk beds are a classic way to provide comfortable sleeping accommodations for young overnight guests.

However, caution needs to be taken with regard to bunk beds: they're easy to fall out of. In assessing whether bunk beds are a good choice for you, take your child's age and personality into account. "Know your own child," says children's-store owner Katharine Tiddens, by way of advice. "I was the kind of child who stood as high as I could on a bed and jumped off." If your child tends to be a daredevil, you might want to rule out bunks. For sleepwalkers, too, bunk

LEFT: Built-in double bunk beds provide a perfect sleeping solution for young guests. The top bunks share a central built-in ladder. The drawers along the base are perfect for storage.

OPPOSITE: Unique metal beds, complete with sky-blue duvets, make a boy's room seem airy and bright. Baseball-themed sheets contribute to this room's playful, sporty mood.

beds are out. But for children who can use them safely, they offer worlds of fun and are great for building forts, among other things. If you decide to purchase bunk beds, consider investing in a pair of twin beds that are made to be stacked, rather than buying a one-piece bunk bed. When your child gets older and decides he or she wants to return to earth, the set can be easily dismantled and turned into matching twin beds.

This sturdy bed from Maine Cottage (see "Resources," page 150) has the advantages of a day bed. It creates an inviting nook for reading and playing, as well as sleeping.

MATTRESSES

Since they sleep more, children spend significantly more time in bed than adults do. You may be tempted to compromise on mattress quality—these are kids after all, and mattresses are surprisingly expensive— but to do so would be a real mistake. Because they're growing, children need extra support when they sleep. As with adult-sized mattresses, the best approach when buying one for a child is to try out different models. Check the return policy of a mattress, just in case it doesn't work for your child. There are a number of fill materials now available for mattresses, from cotton and wool to foam and latex (of which the latter is particularly good for larger children). And, for a child who prefers sleeping on a harder surface, you may want to consider a Japanese-style futon.

BEDDING

What child doesn't want to sleep surrounded by lovable cartoon characters, whether Mickey Mouse or the Lion King? Sheets, pillowcases, and duvet covers are an area where almost any parent can splurge. If it really makes your child happy to sleep on Pokémon sheets—no matter how temporary the fad—you may want to acquiesce. One ten-year-old boy I know, Frederick, sleeps between Boston Red Sox sheets, in Red Sox pajamas, with Red Sox socks on his feet (no need to wonder what city he calls home!). Other children may shy away from logos, choosing bright colors or lively patterns instead. In any case, patterned sheets, which often come with matching comforters or duvet covers, can literally transform a room.

Needless to say, if you live in Alaska or Florida, your requirements for linens will be different. Flannel or jersey sheets are best for frosty winters; plain cotton is coolest for humid summer heat. For blankets and bed covers, similar rules apply. Cotton blankets are best for warm climates, wool blankets for cool ones. Polyester-filled comforters, and duvet covers, are easy to wash and often have sheets to match. Duvets—or down-filled comforters—are wonderfully luxurious. If you select the right thickness for your climate, a duvet should keep your child warm in winter and cool in summer. Ask the salespeople to tell you whether a light-, medium-, or heavyweight duvet is right for your climate. If you live in an area where extremes of temperature are the norm, you may want to choose a light duvet for summer, and a heavier one for winter. Take note, however, that some children are allergic to down, so before splurging on a duvet, you might want to make sure your child is not prone to this particular allergy. (Try letting him or her sleep with a down pillow first; if you don't see any reaction after a week or so, he or she is probably not sensitive to down.)

If you prefer to use blankets on your child's bed, layer them for added warmth, adjusting the number according to the season. It's best to avoid antique quilts or other valuable coverings—these may look charming, but they're a nuisance to launder properly.

As a rule, all children's bedding should be sturdy and easy to clean. If you don't find a comforter or duvet cover in a design that seems right, you and your child can always make your own, using fabric paint and stencils (or forgo the stencils and simply paint free-hand onto the cloth). A great activity for a rainy day!

Children may have stronger ideas about pillows than you ever imagined. Some like them soft, like clouds. Others like the support of something firm beneath their heads. Allow your child to choose his or her pillows—within reason, of course. And why not throw in some extra pillows? They can be invaluable for leaning back against when reading in bed—or in case a pillow fight breaks out.

CLOCKWISE FROM ABOVE: This whimsical chair with cutouts is actually adult-size furniture with a twist.

If space allows, nothing beats the comfort of an easy-chair for reading.

Beanbag chairs have made a come-back. This chair is a scaled down version for kids.

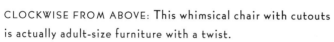

★ CHAIRS

If your kid's room has space for an easy chair, consider it a blessing. A big, comfy chair is the absolute best place in which to read—and snuggle—with your child. An old hand-me-down, overstuffed armchair is perfect. Why not brighten it with a new slipcover and an accent pillow in a contrasting shade? Other chairs will also do. Why not a rocking chair, a fanciful wicker chair, or an exotic chair made of rattan? Beanbag chairs are irresistible to children, as are inflatable ones in lollipop colors. There's even cardboard furniture, too. Not to mention something called the Memo chair, a beanbag-like creation designed by Ron Arad, that adopts the contours of those who sit in it.

Chairs can serve many functions in a child's room: a place to read, to do homework, to snuggle with mom, or provide seating for a special friend—human or otherwise.

the elements

STORAGE

"Keep editing," says designer Kevin Walz, advising how to handle children's seemingly endless collections of toys. Whether it's birthday party favors or substantial Christmas gifts, today's child seems doomed to accumulate. As a parent, keeping your child's things edited and organized has to be a priority. No matter how large his or her room is, without careful and regular pruning it will soon be overrun. Ask yourself (and your kids), "How often do they use this object? Should it be put away for the season? for the day? for the week? forever?"

These cubbies with woven baskets are perfect for holding toys and other small objects. Use muted tones in one color in grown-up spaces, such as living or family rooms. Go brighter for children's rooms, even mixing up colors.

★ SHELVES AND CUBBIES

Keep toys-of-the-moment on low shelves and in accessible open bins; toys that come out less frequently—on rainy days, say, or when cousins visit—should be placed on higher shelves for longer-term storage. Keeping some toys out of sight can be a great strategy, especially for very small children. A toy that's been in a special toy box, or in the back of the closet, for a few months can often, to very young eyes, seem brand-new again.

Children's lives are, more than for the rest of us, in flux. Fad toys can come and go; a doll your daughter loved at age six may be an embarrassment to her when she's ten. The process of paring down your child's toy collection can be a great way to introduce the concept of charity and talk about giving things away so that less-advantaged kids can enjoy them.

For toys that remain, organization is key. "Children want to see their things," says architect Larry Bogdanow. The solution? "Shallow shelves, shallow cabinets, and cubbies." Be creative with storage. Have fun with it. Almost anything can be put to use, including hanging vegetable baskets, plastic buckets, or wicker baskets.

CLOCKWISE FROM TOP LEFT: What was once a humble school locker is transformed into a high-tech-looking—and supremely practical—place for storing toys and other treasures.

The many compartments of this school locker are perfect places to cache childhood treasures.

Colorful paint and a simple stencil transform unfinished wooden boxes into attractive storage.

Labels create instant order. Or try a more visual alternative, such as Polaroid photographs of a drawer or bin's contents. Galvanized storage bins are a perfect way to keep cubbies organized.

Why not store items by size or type or according to your child's very own sorting system? Or, for out-of-the-way storage, invest in some colorful wooden boxes on wheels that can be rolled into a closet or under a bed. A spare bureau can be painted and outfitted with dividers, making it a great place for storing the legions of small toys that can so easily engulf a child's room. For long-term storage, try decorating and personalizing wood or cardboard boxes. Label them with numbers, with Polaroid photos of each drawer's contents, or with shipping tags on colorful strings.

The salespeople at your hardware or furniture store can advise you on the right shelving system for your child's needs. Whatever your choice, be sure to bolt all dressers and shelf units to studs in the wall. Special kits for securing furniture are available at hardware stores and anywhere child-safety products are sold.

ABOVE LEFT: Wire baskets are great for organizing stuffed animals and small toys, while keeping them on display. These baskets were originally used in a public swimming pool's locker room.

ABOVE RIGHT: These woven baskets are inexpensive and add a touch of color.

OPPOSITE: A divided bookshelf filled with various types of storage baskets is an easy and attractive way to organize toys.

project: **Folding Screen with Pockets**

TOOLS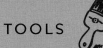

- hot glue gun
- fabric pen
- pinking shears
- square template for pocket
- pins
- needle
- staple gun

MATERIALS

- six 42-inch and six 15-inch wood canvas stretchers
- wood glue
- 1½ yards artists' canvas, or enough to cover a 60-by-150-inch space
- ¼ yard each of three fabrics of contrasting colors (three pieces each measuring at least 10 by 15 inches)
- thread in 3 contrasting colors for sewing pockets
- seam binding, about 3¼ yards for each frame (optional)
- 6 hinges the depth of the stretchers (e.g., ½-inch hinges for ½-inch-deep stretchers)

Here is a kid-sized folding screen, complete with pockets to hold treasures. It can hide little messes or create a private corner, and when the canvas gets dirty, it can be easily replaced. For a different look, eliminate the pockets and prime and paint the canvas. Although a number of steps are necessary, you can start the project in the evening, let the frames dry overnight, and then complete the screen in the morning. Look for the canvas stretchers and artists' canvas at art supply stores.

1 Lay the wood stretchers on the floor, forming three rectangles, and slip the "tongues" into the grooves to form joints. Try different combinations to test the best match, looking for the tightest fit in each case.

2 Pull the joints apart, apply a drop of wood glue to each one, and reassemble. Lay the frame flat to dry, checking to make sure the corners are nicely squared and not lopsided. Allow to dry according to the instructions provided with the glue.

3 Lay the canvas on a flat surface, and place a frame on top of it, positioning it so that it covers about one-third of the fabric. Using the fabric pen, trace around the frame, making the outline about 5 inches larger on all sides. Cut out the traced outline with the pinking shears. Cut out two more pieces in the same manner. Do not worry about making exact measurements, as the excess fabric will be trimmed away later.

4 To create the patch pocket, place the square template you have chosen on one of the three pieces of fabric of contrasting colors. Trace around it with the fabric pen. Now rotate the template 45 degrees and trace the point on top. The finished shape should resemble a house with a roof. Cut out the shape with the pinking shears, and repeat with the remaining two pieces of colored fabric.

5 Pin each pocket in position on a panel of the canvas. Using a decorative stitch and thread in a contrasting color, top-stitch the pockets in place on the sides and bottom, leaving the top open and the flap ("roof") free to fall forward.

6 Lay the three canvas panels on a flat surface. Center a frame on top of each panel. Using the glue gun, tack the canvas to each frame in the top two corners.

7 Turn over each frame and attach canvas and, using the staple gun, staple the fabric to the back of the frame. Start at the center of each of the four sides and pull the fabric taut as you work toward the ends.

8 Using the pinking shears, trim off the excess canvas.

9 If desired, use the hot glue gun to cover the staples and canvas edge with seam binding.

10 To assemble the screen, lay two of the panels face down, with two long edges next to each other, keeping in mind which end is the top (check for the open end of the pockets). Holding the panels together, attach them to each other with two of the hinges, positioning one hinge several inches from the top and then the other one the same distance from the bottom. Fold the now-hinged screen flat, and lay the third panel, face down, on top of the stack. (Again, keep in mind the position of the pocket.) Attach the remaining two hinges along the edges of the top two panels, placing them on the side opposite the original hinges, so the screen will fold accordion fashion.

ABOVE: A captain's bed providing generous storage is tucked next to the closet, which has simple, chunky wood handles. The built-ins and graphic use of repeated rectangles and squares create unity in this small but well planned room.

LEFT: This extra-solid built-in desk and shelves are perfect for accommodating a young boy's essential possessions, from team photos to video games to books.

story: **Captain's Quarters**

Instead of living in a house, architect Josh Schweitzer and his family reside in a series of "pods"—structures that are connected to each other only by paths through fresh air. Every five years, they add a new pod to their sprawling residence. One year, it was seven-year-old Declan's turn to have a new room. The boy's pod is painted green, in part to match the tropical-looking banana trees that grow just outside his windows.

In Declan's room, for which Josh Schweitzer designed all the furniture and cabinetry, there's no limit to the great storage options. The captain's bed has six built-in drawers, two for toys and four for clothes. The desk area is just the right size for a computer. Even more fun, from a child's point of view, are the Dutch doors, which open onto the outdoors. With the upper, lower, or even both doors ajar, his pod is always connected to nature.

The floating shelf above the bed is perfect for books; the stacked plastic bins and small unit with transparent drawers—both available from hardware stores—are indispensable for storing small objects.

★ CLOSETS

CLOCKWISE FROM TOP LEFT: An armoire adds closet space in an unused corner of this boy's room.

An adjustable closet system is a practical idea for a child's room; its components can be changed and rearranged as his or her storage requirements evolve.

Decorative drawer pulls are a great way to add life to plain furniture. Here, old wooden puzzle pieces have been recycled into drawer pulls.

A child's closet should have a child-height clothes rod. If necessary, have the closet's existing rod lowered so your child can reach it, and add a second one, placed high in the closet, for out-of-season or infrequently worn clothes. At the beginning of each season, rotate winter and summer clothes, so that your child can always reach that season's clothes. Modular custom closets make great storage systems for kids, since they can always be adjusted to meet changing needs. Other good storage solutions include zip-up canvas wardrobes, which come in a variety of shapes and sizes. For easy access to everyday clothes, place a set of pegs at kid height either in the child's room or near the entrance to your house or apartment. This way, kids can easily grab or hang up their essentials, from a parka to a baseball cap, on their way in or out of the house, without bothering with finding a hanger.

WORK AND PLAY AREAS

Children require a place to work and crave a place to escape. Nurture your child's creative needs by providing a kid-size table and chairs and plenty of art supplies. Help the students in your life meet their academic commitments by creating a homework haven complete with desk, chair, and components for their computer. Cultivate children's imaginations by building them a personal sanctuary—a homemade fort, a diminutive playhouse, or a cozy corner can fulfill their dream of having a personalized hideaway that they can call their very own.

This playroom, which is shared by two children, has lots of storage (both open and hidden), attractive vintage furniture, and a lively "carpet" that's actually made of linoleum.

★ DESKS

Homework may seem onerous to your children, but they still need a surface on which to do it. If your four-year-old wants a desk to work at, bear in mind that, in a few short years, she will outgrow it. When children reach middle-school age, and schoolwork becomes more serious, it's time to invest in a serious desk, preferably one that can serve when the child reaches adulthood, too. No desk can be too big, says designer Laura Bohn. "By the time kids have computers and printers, the desk space gets used up." Even if you're not in the market for such a mammoth piece of furniture, be sure to choose one that can hold a computer but also has space for writing and other non-computer activities.

No desk can ever be too large. This cantilevered one can accommodate group projects, with children working side by side.

The proper location of the desk requires careful consideration. It's fine to position it so that the student looks directly out of a window or sits perpendicular to one, but be sure that light isn't streaming directly onto the monitor screen, which can cause eyestrain. Also, pay close attention to the height of the monitor on the desk. Your child should be looking down into the screen, but only slightly. Taking such simple precautions should help prevent repetitive stress and other computer-related injuries.

It's easy to underestimate the importance of a good desk chair. An adjustable ergonomic chair is best for use at a desk. The highest-quality ones have adjustable backs and springy seats that can be lowered or raised. Don't skimp on this—your child is growing, and the quality of a child's desk chair can affect his or her posture and body alignment in adulthood.

★ PLAY AREAS

Every child needs a place where he or she can create and display crafts, sprawl with a book on the floor, or finger paint without having to worry about ruining the carpet. Ideally, there should be space to leave works-in-progress, whether they're Lego houses or homemade forts. An indoor play area is one space where children's furniture really is perfect: a small table and chairs, or perhaps a futon couch, should be all that is needed.

Outdoor play areas can be almost limitless in their possibilities for fun. Almost any small outdoor structure can be transformed into a hideaway, to be enjoyed by both children and adults. Enlist your child's help in transforming a storage shed, building a tree house, or assembling a gazebo from a kit. Some families, apartment dwellers in particular, do not have the luxury of a separate play area, inside or out. In cases where a playroom has multiple uses—it may double as a family TV room, for example—an effective storage solution is of key importance. In play areas where siblings have both shared and personal toys, the latter can be stored in cupboards or baskets for each child.

The play area here is both spacious and efficient, with low shelves and child-sized table and chairs.

ABOVE: Every child longs for a place of his or her own; with its numerous, wonderful details, this playhouse is ideal. Note the shutters with heart cutouts, the Dutch door, and play chimney.

LEFT: A playfully harmless "big bad wolf" sculpture (made of painted wood) guards the playhouse with an enormous grin.

project: **Play Tablecloth**

TOOLS

- pinking shears
- drill with small bit
- hole punch for use with paper

MATERIALS

- vinyl or oilcloth in the color or pattern of your choice and large enough to allow an 8-inch drape on each side
- assorted plastic charms (cake decorations or decorative magnets with the magnet removed), as many as desired
- 4 pieces colored string at least 8 inches long

This tablecloth is a colorful way to protect a table from paint spills and other art-related accidents.

1 Measure and cut the cloth with pinking shears—allow for a generous drape off the edge of the table.

2 If necessary, carefully drill a hole in the plastic charms for threading the string.

3 Punch holes at about 1 inch in from the edges of the fabric, using the hole punch. (For a smaller hole, try using a leather punch, available at craft-supply stores.)

4 Thread a string through the hole in one of the plastic charms, then through one of the holes in the fabric, and tie so that the charm dangles from the edge. Repeat for each hole.

story: **Meet Me in the Middle**

Nine-year-old Maxine and her five-year-old brother, Henry, enjoy the luxury of having an entire wing all to themselves, which includes their bedrooms—hers is coral pink, his is Delft blue—and an innovative triangular play area. Here, the children engage in every form of play, from staging puppet shows to playing tiddlywinks to banging away on xylophones and drums. Their mother, architect Valerie Boom, organized the space like a school, with lots of shelves and cubbies for storage. Books, puzzles, toys, and games are kept on open shelves. A computer/television screen on one shelf is hooked up to the living room television for parental monitoring. "We can decide when it's time for *Sesame Street* or a videotape," Boom says. The playroom is both attractive and practical. Its wood floor has been bleached and polyurethaned, so that when the children spill paint and other substances, the mess is easily cleaned up. This is a space designed for fun. Even so, certain rules apply, aimed at keeping the area tidy and clean. Food and drink are forbidden in the wing, and shoes are not to be worn in the space.

ABOVE: In the play area between the children's bedrooms, toys and books are kept in low, colorful, school-style cabinets.

OPPOSITE: The siblings' rooms open out onto a common play area.

The children's bedrooms, which measure 8 by 14 feet, have natural sisal carpeting, with area rugs placed over it for coziness and color. Although the rooms are relatively small, their ceilings are high—more than 11 feet. Set above each child's bed is a loft that measures about 7 feet from the floor. These are carpeted, with a single mattress for sleepovers. The children climb up to the lofts using wooden library ladders on wheels. Safety has never been a problem. "Nobody has ever fallen down," Boom reports.

Furnishings are minimal but carefully chosen. The bureau, nightstand, and French manor dollhouse in Maxine's room, still in their original paint, were Boom's own furniture during her childhood in Holland, designed by Maxine's grandmother. The furniture in Henry's room is simple but imaginative. There's a blue wooden table, with metal legs, designed by Boom, with a longer set of legs to be added when he grows taller. Toy airplanes hang from the ceiling. Henry uses the bright rubber mat with punch-out numbers on the floor to launch rockets or create islands surrounded by toy boats.

"Her" room is pink. Although not very large, it has the benefit of high ceilings. It also has ample storage in the form of built-in shelving, with a rolling library ladder for access.

"His" room is blue, an exact duplicate of his sister's, right down to the shelving and the library ladder. The library ladder rolls easily from one side of the shelves to another. Because of it, even toys and books stored up high can be easily reached.

★ COZY SPACES

OPPOSITE: Using an eclectic mix of fabrics, a grown-up's love seat gets a new life in a cozy place in this girl's room.

ABOVE: An assortment of pastel-colored pillows invites a nap on this bed built into a nook next to the picture window.

Children crave privacy, and they love having a secret territory that's all their own. They adore hiding places—under tables, in closets, behind sofas. A cozy corner appeals to all these desires. Most kids want a personal space within their own room, a place where they can curl up and just be themselves. This kind of space can take many forms, from a large, comfy easy-chair to a corner equipped with throw pillows and an upholstered foam mattress (also handy for sleepovers). You can even build an elaborate fantasy corner, complete with canopy, or use a folding screen to create a separate corner for reading, writing, or dreaming. Mosquito netting can be hung from a round frame on the ceiling, thereby creating a magical, diaphanous tent—why not? And colorful, plastic-beaded curtains are another funky, fantastical way to divide space.

story:

Maya's Room

For her rustic bedroom, ten-year-old Maya Bogdanow had three wishes. One of these was fulfilled, the other two were negotiated. First, she wanted a beaded curtain. She had seen one at a friend's house and became enchanted by its glittering plastic jewels— bright, and unabashedly fake—including amethysts, rubies, and topazes. She loved the gentle clicking sound the beads made as she passed through them, and she loved the air of mystery they brought to the room. In this particular case, her wish was her parents' command. They happily bought her three bright beaded curtains at approximately twelve dollars each, hanging them on a track above the door to her room.

Maya also wanted a purple room—but here her parents balked, sure that her small, dark room would look oppressive in that shade. So they offered a compromise. They suggested a lavender room—

a whisper of purple, rather than a shout. And they complemented the shade with delicately hued pastels, including a pale purple bedspread. They also painted her playroom, adjacent to the bedroom, in very light blue.

Maya's third wish was that the light-filled family study also be painted blue, but this her father declined. He explained to his daughter that when sunlight enters a blue room, the color can seem gray, making the room seem dark. So the family chose to brighten the study instead by painting it a pale butter yellow.

For Maya's furniture, her parents wanted flexibility above all. They created built-in adjustable shelving; toys are stored on these open shelves, while Maya's impressive collection of Beanie Babies is nestled in a large wicker basket. It was her idea to string her

shiny blue and red horseback-riding ribbons across the room, securing them at each wall, just below ceiling height. In the study, which is shared by both children and adults, Maya's parents elected to use a standard-height table. But they made sure that it would be accessible to their daughter, too, by pairing it with an adjustable chair.

ABOVE: Hung from the entrance arch of the sleeping alcove, the plastic-beaded curtains separate the bed from the play area.

OPPOSITE: Jewel-like plastic beads are an inexpensive—and undeniably colorful—way to divide a room.

★ PERSONAL TOUCHES

A child's bedroom is his or her life, in a sense. Every child wants to have a space to display art, photographs, or blue ribbons. You can section off a wall and give it over to display by hanging a board of magnetic stainless steel, enameled steel, cork, or recycled rubber. An old-fashioned display board is simple to make and a great way to show off some of these treasures. To make one, take a piece of cardboard, wrap it in cotton batting, then cover it with fabric, stapling it from the back so that the material is taut. Stretch ribbons diagonally at equal intervals across the board, and staple them at the back so that the ribbons are taut. Then create a crisscross effect by weaving more ribbons, on the opposite diagonal,

Personalize a child's room with colorfully printed wooden blocks spelling out his or her name.

in and out of the first set of ribbons, and then stapling the new ones at the back so they are also stretched taut. For added interest, sew buttons or bows on the board at the places where the crisscrossing ribbons meet. Exhibit your child's favorite photographs, baseball cards, drawings, and the like on the display board by tucking them under the ribbons.

Another great display idea is to screw a metal strip into the wall at about chair-rail height. Then, using magnets or Lucite photo frames with magnetic backing (available at drug and photo stores), you can create an ongoing rotating gallery. As for filling the frames, that's easy. Thanks to color photocopying, almost anything can end up on the wall, from a special birthday card from a friend to pictures of beloved small objects such as bird feathers and tiny shells. Taken apart and framed, your child's favorite calendar

TOOLS

- tape measure
- pencil
- sheet of tracing paper
- fabric pen
- scissors
- hot glue gun
- handsaw
- electric drill
- hammer
- mat knife
- metal ruler
- small nails

MATERIALS

- 9-by-12-inch felt pieces in the colors of your choice (available from craft or fabric stores; see step one for the number of pieces you'll need)
- piece of cardboard
- tassels or pom-poms (available from fabric or craft-supply stores) in colors that coordinate—or contrast nicely—with the felt. You'll need enough tassels or pom-poms to provide one per point.
- ¼-inch-thick wood furring strips (available at lumber yards and hardware stores; see step one for the length you'll need).

project: Circus Pennant Border

1 Measure all the walls of your child's room from corner to corner to determine the amount of felt you'll need for a border that goes around the entire room. You should use one felt square for every 18 inches of wall space. Each sheet of felt will yield four pennants, 4½ by 6 inches in size. (You should also use the wall measurements to calculate the length of the wood strips you will need.)

2 Trace one of the pennant shapes on page 97 on tracing paper, enlarging it to be 6" high from bottom to point, and use it to create a cardboard template. Using a fabric marker, draw the outline of your template four times on each piece of felt, following the diagram at right. Repeat until you have drawn enough pennant shapes to go around the entire room.

3 Cut out the pennants along the outlines, being careful to keep the felt smooth and not to stretch it.

4 Using the glue gun, attach the tassels to the points on the underside (where your pencil lines were).

5 On a floor or counter, measure and cut the furring strips to fit the length of the walls, subtracting the thickness of the strip itself (approximately ¼ inch) from the overall length.

6 Pre-drill small pilot holes in the wood every 3 feet or so—these are where you will nail the strips to the walls.

7 Glue the pennants, in the color sequence of your choice, onto each strip, making sure the top edge aligns with the top of the wood and that the sides of each pennant touch the sides of the neighboring pennants, without overlapping.

8 Nail the strips to the walls through the pre-drilled holes, making sure the strips are level with the floor and ceiling.

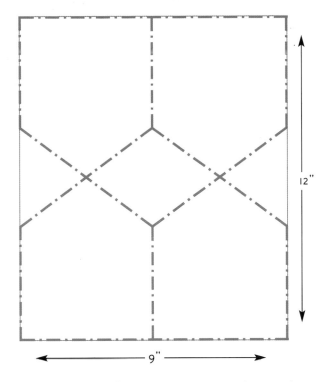

can be put into use for years to come. Why not frame a sentimental letter from your child's grandmother, or create a blow-up of his or her favorite trading cards?

Just about anything can be used to make a fun picture on your child's wall. And inexpensive picture frames can be found almost anywhere, from dime stores on up, and they can be arranged in numerous artful ways. Try mounting nine identical frames in a grid pattern. Or try buying the same frame in different complementary colors. You can always repaint old frames, then mix and match them with others in the same or contrasting colors.

Everyone, young and old, wants to leave his own imprint on his living space. Your child can do this in numerous ways, from picking colors and fabrics to creating artwork and other decorations. A toy box decorated with the child's handprints, or a footprint step stool, pro-

vide a way for him or her to make a truly personal mark on his or her environment, while marking the passage of time as little hands and feet grow bigger.

Kids are artists by nature, and parents should get creative right along with them. There are boundless quantities of projects you can undertake together. Shell and rock collections can be glued onto the edges of a picture frame or mirror frame. Sand, glitter, and found treasures can be added to the outside of a plain box, making it special. Paper lanterns (no bulbs needed) and party decorations, hung from the walls or ceiling, can make any room fun. Why not start with the door to your child's room? Most kids like having their name on it. Help him or her to spell it out in creative ways, using magnetic letters or appliqués, for example. That way, no one can forget that this is Zack or Anna's room.

project: **Handprint Switch Plate**

TOOLS

- small paintbrush
- masking tape

MATERIALS

- wooden switch plate—
  sanded, primed, and painted
  with desired color
- drop cloth
- white paper or artist's palette
- latex or poster paint in
  3 colors
- damp paper towels for cleanup

Virtually all you need to make this simple project are a wooden switch plate, some bright paints, and your child's willing hand.

❶ Remove the existing switch plate and replace with a primed and painted switch plate.

❷ With masking tape, tape off a rectangle around the switch plate.

❸ Spread a thick, even layer of paint on the white paper or artist's palette.

❹ Have your child press his palm into the paint, then use additional white paper to blot the paint one time.

❺ With spread fingers, press palm onto the switch plate. (Your child may need your help with keeping her hand steady and fingers apart.)

❻ After the paint on the switch plate dries, use contrasting poster paint or finger paints to fill in the gaps.

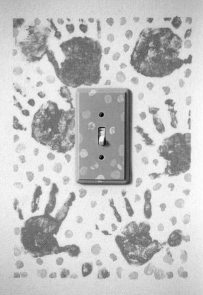

Galvanized-Metal Magnet Board

A shiny, modern look for a display board—galvanized metal can be purchased from a home center and mounted onto a wall or closet door to create a super-sized magnet board. Because metal edges can be sharp, make sure the panel is set into the recess of the door, or has no edges that are exposed to little hands. You can use assorted fanciful, decorative magnets to attach artwork, photos, and ephemera.

BELOW: A footprint is incorporated into the fanciful design of this hand-painted stool.

Graham Horvath, seven years old, collects fossils, autographed baseballs, and toy knights. He reads medieval tales, watches the videotape of "Camelot" over and over again, and loves to fish. His bedroom is where he has lived since he was born and whose character—the placement of the desk, pegs, and armoire—has not changed in seven years. Only the size of the furniture and the kinds of toys and objects has shifted. "Graham's an old soul," said his mother, Michelle Horvath, a stylist who lives in Montclair, New Jersey, with her husband, Wayne, and their daughter, Hannah, age nine.

When the Horvaths bought the 1840s house, just before Graham was born, his room had four bare walls. It was plain. To give the room instant character, Ms. Horvath transformed one wall by applying wainscoting topped with a shelf for collections that didn't yet exist, but would work as a picture rail, a place to put baby pictures, family photos, and a teddy bear or two.

It is the room of a collector. Bleached fox skulls, one big, the other little, a bear claw, a bear tooth, and a fulsome set of shark's teeth are centered on the desk top. Antlers are mounted on a wall, as is a framed poster of fish. On a bureau top, miniature

knights are ready to charge into combat. A row of autographed baseballs, including one from Yogi Berra, line a shelf, while below are pegs holding Graham's collection of baseball caps, and beneath that, another set of pegs holds yet more baseball caps. A wallpaper border of cowboys and Indians runs across the top of the wall, adding a bit of whimsy.

What's visible is only part of Graham's many collections. In his desk, a friend's castaway, are drawers divided into tiny compartments, and each divider holds another collection. "Graham likes old lighters that don't work, knives, and the bones of fish," his mother said. Every piece of furniture and shelf is a testament to one of Graham's passions—and to sentimental family memories. Each year, his grandparents give him a Hess truck, and they line up on a high shelf. His father's college wrestling trophies are on another shelf. Generations of family life, reflected in objects and furniture, warm the room.

Only the sleigh bed, bought when Graham was three, was a new piece of furniture, and it was chosen for its sturdiness. Now its scratches and marks make it look like a near-instant antique.

OPPOSITE: On the top of an antique bureau, some old lead soldiers gather their forces for battle.

ABOVE: From the old-fashioned frieze, at ceiling height, to the vintage marionette by the bed, this young boy's bedroom has an old-world feel.

RIGHT: An assortment of antlers, fox skulls, and sharks' teeth reveal this to be the desk of a budding anthropologist.

great rooms

What makes a room great? Ingenuity? Functionality? How about sheer playfulness? All three of these elements, I think, need to be present to make a great room for a child. In the right proportions, they can add up to magic.

The best of these rooms take a practical approach, but they also let whimsy rule. In every case, the people who designed them—whether parents or professional designers—asked the children about their wants and needs before sitting down to design. And their interest shows in these rooms, which appeal to parents and their offspring alike. Great rooms can happen anywhere. No matter where they're located, in an urban loft, a country cottage, or a suburban bungalow, they have imagination and fun in common. The beauty of these rooms is that they were done on a wide range of budgets, yet the spaces seem equally effective. Especially when seen through the eyes of a child.

LOG
CABIN
RETREAT

When Billy and Timmy Ford head off into their very own log cabin, they're not deep in the forest—as they usually pretend to be—but in an alcove off one of their bedrooms. Even so, this space seems so rustic that it's easy to imagine mountain cats, black bears, and rattlesnakes prowling around outside.

The cabin is the creation of Laura Bohn, an architectural designer. To enter this 10-by-10-foot raw-cedar structure, you have to pass through two doors: the first is standard height, and the second reaches about $4\frac{1}{2}$ feet—a great way to keep adults at bay. "And that's the fun of it," the designer says. Inside,

The cedar cabin is ready for playtime when homework is done.

LEFT: Thanks to a pulley system, the propellers and other parts of this kinetic wall sculpture move at will.

ABOVE: In the playhouse, orange-colored walls and dark-green window trim work perfectly with the camouflage pattern.

OPPOSITE: To reach the loft bed above the door, the playhouse's young residents clamber up the metal rungs on either side.

the cabin glows with warmth, since the walls are painted a brilliant orange, a color chosen by Timmy. The window frames are painted an olive green, to match the prevailing camouflage design. To reach the camouflaged loft bed, the children climb up rungs installed in the wall. The panels at the windows are covered in a wild-animal print. Although the log cabin looks permanent, the designer made sure it could change with the times. If and when the boys outgrow it, the facade can be easily removed. But, for now, that moment seems very far away.

PURPLE POWER

Emily Gibson, ten years old, so loves purple that she wanted every wall of her bedroom painted in that hue. Her mother, an interior designer, gently demurred, "I thought it would be too much," she says. So mother and daughter compromised, creating a whole palette of pale, soothing colors instead. Now, in Emily's room, there are two walls in aqua, two in yellow-green, and a headboard, a comforter cover, and a rug in shades of lavender.

For this room's purple-loving inhabitant, a deep-colored valance, bedcover, and plastic chair in that color. The soft-blue ragged walls soften these intense color accents.

The room's design began with a carpet: a lavender one with a spiral center that Emily had seen in a catalog. She was also bowled over by a pair of curtains—sheer chartreuse polka-dot silk curtains with an aqua-colored cotton lining—that Emily's mother and her partner were making for a client. Since there was some fabric left over, Emily was able to have a pair of her own for her room. The palette—blue, green, and lavender—slowly emerged. Emily's mother created a contour border detail on the lavender headboard with dark chartreuse velveteen. She also used this material for the bed skirt and for the center of the flower appliqué on the lavender bedcover. On the floor, blue wall-to-wall carpet complements Emily's much-loved area rug, which is itself perfectly compatible with the appliqué on the bed. The cornice box above the window echoes the shape of the headboard, only upside down. For a final touch of purple (can there ever be enough?), Emily's mother gave the room a touch of whimsy in the form of a deep-lavender inflatable chair.

FROM TOP: This colorful bedcover is surprisingly easy to make. (See "Flower-Appliquéd Comforter Cover," page 111.)

The flower-shaped drawer pull echoes the room's floral-patterned carpet and bedcover.

Add color and charm by decorating the light switches with your children's designs.

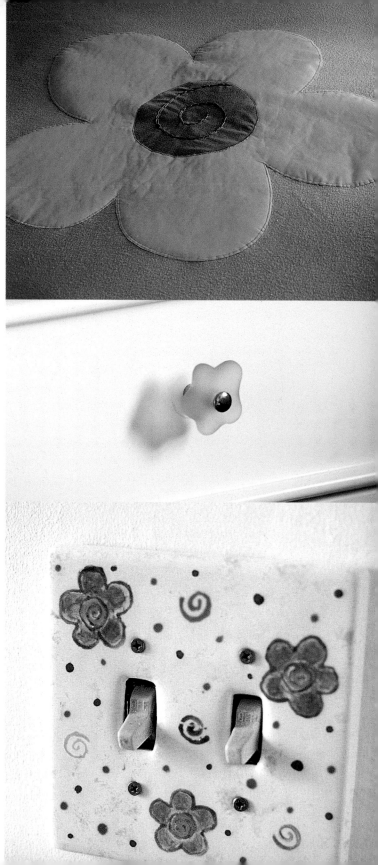

project: Flower-Appliquéd Comforter Cover

TOOLS

- tape measure
- scissors
- pins
- pencil
- sewing machine with zigzag-stitch capability
- compass (for drawing circles)
- embroidery needle

MATERIALS

- 5 yards of 52-inch-wide fleece
- newspaper
- 1¼ yards of standard-width blue velveteen
- ¼ yard of standard-width chartreuse velveteen
- embroidery floss
- white or colored sheet, full size (for lining)
- 10 inches of ¾-inch-wide Velcro, cut into five 2-inch strips
- thread (color should match that of the fleece)

Follow these instructions to make a full-size comforter.

1 Cut the fleece in half to make two equal pieces, each 2½ yards in length.

2 Cut one of these pieces in half to create two 26-inch-wide panels.

3 Pin the two smaller panels of fleece lengthwise to either side of the outside edge, then sew it together with a ½-inch seam allowance.

4 To create the appliqué, tape two pieces of newspaper together. Draw a flower shape in the size of your choice on the newspaper to use as a pattern, pin it to the blue velveteen, and carefully cut out the flower.

5 Pin the flower in the center of the fleece assembly and sew it on, using a zigzag stitch along its outer edge. Running the zigzag stitch onto the fleece will help finish the velveteen and discourage fraying.

6 For the center of the flower, draw a 9-inch-diameter circle onto the newspaper using the compass as a guide.

7 Pin the circle pattern onto the chartreuse velveteen and cut it out. Pin, then zigzag-stitch the circle onto the center of the flower.

8 To create the decorative center, lightly pencil on a design. Using embroidery floss, chain-stitch the design on the center. It is not necessary to penetrate all layers.

9 Complete the comforter cover by trimming the top layer to the size of the sheet (approximately 90 by 90 inches). Put the right sides of the sheet and the top layer together and stitch the edges of three sides with a ½-inch seam allowance, leaving the bottom end open. Turn right side out.

10 On the open end, turn the exposed edges under ½-inch and top-stitch.

11 To create the closure: evenly space the five Velcro strips along the opening, and pin them in place (measure carefully to ensure that the strips line up well). Stitch around the perimeter of each strip using a thread that matches the fabric.

HERS
AND
HERS

Marlena Hurlbut, age seven, and her sister, Isabella, age four, were born to a mother who is a stylist, an antique collector, and a woman with a strong fantasy life.

So the girls live in practical fairy-tale rooms, where pink-and-white dust ruffles brush the floor, lace christening gowns hang, gossamer-like, from wooden pegs, and carved wooden rabbits are poised along the ledge of a wainscoted wall. The girls thrive in their mother's fantasy designs. What frees them to scoot

The gingham-edged curtains and dust ruffle unify a room full of hand-me-downs and flea-market treasures. Even the newer things here, such as the white curtains, seem deliberately old-fashioned.

TOP: Antique wooden blocks spell out the name of a very modern girl. Such small but personal decorative touches can be found at the top of the wainscoting throughout the room.

LEFT: Antique baby rattles, tied with new silk ribbon, are used as decorative accessories in this girl's room.

OPPOSITE: The antique prints over the bed are casually decorated with a wide ribbon and an old-fashioned baby bonnet. Wainscoting provides the appropriate backdrop for the cottage-style bed and nightstand.

about barefoot, grab a toy from here and there, and clamber up a hand-painted stool decorated with their own footprints is that their mother, Lorraine Hurlbut, designed the fanciful rooms with practicality in mind. Although the rooms are filled with antiques, "I never said you can't play with things," said Ms. Hurlbut. As quintessentially pretty as the rooms are, they are also functional. The rooms are proof that modern little girls can run about unfettered in a turn-of-the-century setting.

When Marlena was born, Ms. Hurlbut chose the color scheme—pink and white—but made the pink-and-white-checked dust ruffle oversized and extra deep, so that when Marlena moved from the crib to a twin bed, the dust ruffle would fit the larger bed. The fabric is also used to trim the white cotton curtains. What prevents the pink-and-white check from being overly cute is its scale. The pattern is big, bold, and graphic. To cover the bed, Ms. Hurlbut found green-and-pink-flowered cotton at a fabric sale, and had it custom-made into a duvet cover.

Everywhere, Ms. Hurlbut has displayed her daughters' favorite possessions in still lifes that are both useful and decorative. Teddy bears, wound with silk ribbon, dangle from pegs by Marlena's bed. Each night, Marlena reaches up and takes the teddy bear of the moment to sleep with her. On the opposite side of the room, Ms. Hurlbut hung Marlena's favorite party dresses—fragile creations of lace, organdy, and dotted swiss—on pegs. Sterling-silver baby rattles nestle together, a reminder of another moment.

An oversized stuffed chair, an old dollhouse, and assorted frilly
dresses, hung as decorations, all contribute to this room's
antique charm. Vintage floral fabric, hung from curtain rods,
makes an eye-catching and distinctive window covering. Above
the window, an old valance is put to use as a shelf.

The wood floors are bare, warm to the feet, and free of rugs—and of dust.

In a highly decorated room, the open floor is an oasis for play. When Isabella was born, she inherited her mother's pink-white-and-green color scheme. For Isabella's room, her parents found 1920s cottage furniture in a soft, muted green. For curtains, Ms. Hurlbut tossed panels of vintage fabric, the ends unfinished, over the curtain rod, for a casually voluptuous look that also does not get in the way of the air conditioner. Isabella's favorite stuffed animals are in her former rocking cradle, canopied by an antique pillow cover.

In both daughters' rooms, there's a place for a bedtime glass of milk and a plate of cookies. Isabella has a green tin tray, and Marlena a silver one.

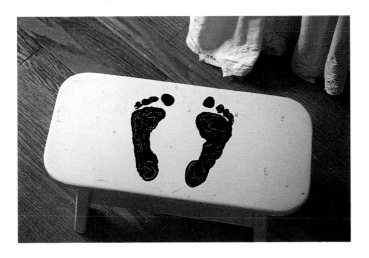

ABOVE: On a marble-topped, hand-painted chest of drawers are a soft velvet hat on a hat stand and photographs from an earlier life.

LEFT: In the most romantic of bedrooms, a real-life, contemporary detail: a footprint-decorated, hand-painted stool.

GOODNIGHT ROOM

When Will Smith was just a year old, his mother, Cathy Smith, who owns a store called Goodnight Room, decorated his room in blue and green, colors that reminded her of nature. Will's mother loves vintage things and her son's room is an artful combination of stylish older elements (including the purplish curtains, with their red taxis and trucks), and items that, while new, have a vintage feel.

Simple, clean-lined furniture and bright compatible colors give this room an inviting warmth. The bed is from Goodnight Room (see "Resources," page 150).

A classic example is the old-fashioned rocket-patterned bedside lamp shade. The centerpiece of the room is the handsome blue bed (designed by Smith and her brother, Stephen Swinhart), a classic camp bed with a star cutout in the headboard (to match her son's "shining personality," she says). A comfy blue-chambray beanbag completes the room.

Smith found smart solutions for storage, using an old terrarium to house her son's seashell collection, for example. The open green cubby, in which toys are kept, is "reminiscent of toy cubbies you'd find in a kindergarten classroom," says Smith.

TOP RIGHT: This paper lamp shade, decorated with space-ships, can be easily reproduced. Just buy the stamps of your choice, then apply them by hand to a plain paper shade.

BOTTOM RIGHT: The vintage material has a fire-engine theme. The curtains are hung on thick wooden hooks, which are both attractive and easy for a child to open and close.

OPPOSITE: A divided bookshelf filled with various types of storage baskets is an easy and attractive way to organize toys. The retro-looking green of this unit works beautifully with the blue bed and bright patterned curtains. An old terrarium makes a great home for a seashell collection.

CENTER STAGE

At night, six-year-old Greta must dream of India. The raised bed she sleeps in is worthy of a princess from that fabled country. The wonderfully bright, imaginative, silvery, wooden bed is raised high off the floor. Its raw silk canopy, in a yellow-tinged chartreuse, is edged in red tassels and trimmed with tiny silver charms. Red roses brighten the corners of the canopy, and its lining is dotted with golden stars. "Greta wanted to look up at the sky," her mother says. Now, each night, she does.

Silver-painted wood and a tasseled canopy decorate an elaborate bed that would suit a princess.

The bed, which was designed by the architecture/ design team of D. D. Allen and Michael Pierce, is versatile too. The reversible bedspread has red-and-white-striped velvet on one side, and a leaf design on the other. And if Greta wants to transform her bed into a theater, she has only to pull the canopy's sheer cotton batiste curtains shut, and then open them again, so that the show can begin.

For the walls, Greta's mother cut out huge red roses from a roll of vintage wallpaper and used them to create a floral border around the room. She took the garden trellis in the wallpaper design as inspiration, painting a real wooden trellis green, then attaching it to the wall. On it, she hung treasured pieces from her daughter's handbag collection, including some from the Civil War, and newer ones, including a bag made of fluffy pink material. Even the step stool that Greta uses to climb into bed has a floral theme: a rose is painted on the bottom step, and her name is painted on the top step.

TOP RIGHT: This enchanting bed can be transformed into a Far East sanctuary by closing the diaphanous curtains.

BOTTOM RIGHT: A hand-painted, personalized footstool makes it easy to climb in and out of the high-canopied bed.

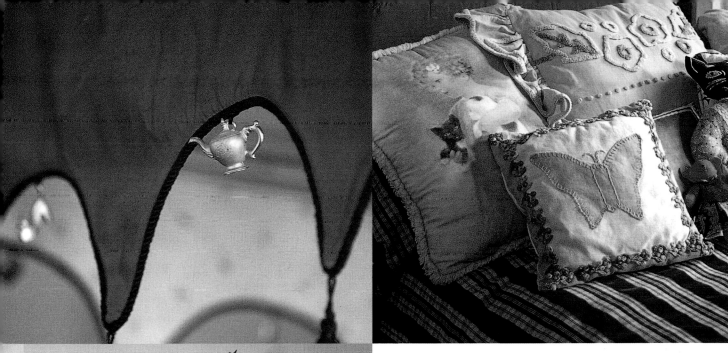

ABOVE LEFT: The scalloped canopy is accented with silver charms.

ABOVE RIGHT: A mix of antique pillowslips and toys add a touch of childlike charm.

Trellis Display

A painted garden trellis is an imaginative way to store and organize this young girl's handbag collection. Fancy drawer pulls can be used to decorate the wooden pegs of the trellis. Sand, prime, and paint the trellis in the color (or colors!) of your choice, then screw it to the wall at child's height.

HISTORY LESSON

"We designed this to be kind of a tree house," designer Sasha Emerson says of her six-year-old daughter Sophie's room. With its generous wraparound windows, this space affords wonderful views of the surrounding forest. In her design, Emerson played upon the abundance of natural light and greenery. She conceived the room in earth tones, adding a duvet cover with what she calls a "sunny Kodacolor vintage look," a green-and-white wool blanket, and a bright floral-patterned rug.

Wraparound windows allow light to flood into this tree-house—inspired room.

Emerson consulted her daughter when selecting the contents of her room but was careful to limit her choices. "If it were completely up to her," Emerson says, "she'd have Barbie sheets." In the absence of Barbie, mid-twentieth-century modernism permeates the room. "I found almost everything in the room at the flea market," Emerson says. The 1950s light fixture "was originally cheap metal, sprayed gold. I painted it blue, red, and yellow." The Heywood-Wakefield bookshelf dates from sometime between the 1930s and the 1950s. Above it, there's a 1940s children's kite, framed in maple to match the pale wood of the bookshelf. Both the vanity and the

matching chest of drawers were designed by mid-twentieth-century designer Gilbert Rohde. The portrait of a young girl above the chest dates from 1931. The globe-shaped banks on the vanity are part of an ever-expanding collection—mother and daughter both love to scour flea markets for these special treasures.

Not everything here is second-hand. The striking 1-by-1-foot chest, which Sophie uses as a jewelry box, was bought at an unfinished wood store by her aunt, who then painted it in bright colors, adding colorful, contrasting knobs.

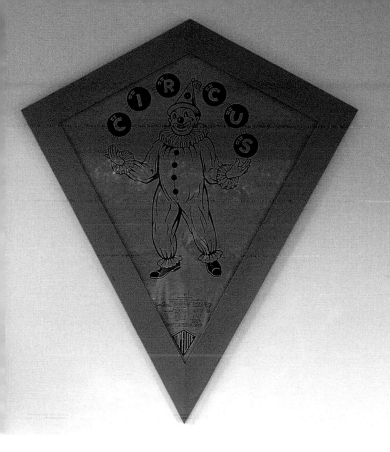

TOP ROW FROM LEFT TO RIGHT: An unfinished wooden chest of drawers was painted in several colors, then contrasting drawer pulls in various shapes and sizes were added.

Thanks to a new coat of paint, this unusual, old overhead light was given a second life.

An antique kite is framed in its own shape to become an original piece of wall art.

This mid-nineteenth-century chest of drawers, designed by Gilbert Rohde, is topped by an old globe and other vintage finds.

RIGHT: Both mother and daughter share an enthusiasm for old globe-shaped banks, frequently picking up new additions to the collection at flea markets and garage sales.

BEDTIME STORIES

"The idea was to enchant," artist Joan Albright says of her decision to paint her daughter Nicola's room. And paint she did, creating elaborate murals populated by a magical menagerie of animals, on three of the walls. Above five-year-old Nicola's headboard there's a fanciful nocturnal scene of a rooster sleeping on the back of an antlered deer. Nearby, two rabbits are riding on a black horse. On the wall above the footboard—the first thing Nicola sees upon

The Hitchcock bed, a family heirloom, works beautifully with the decorative murals on the walls around it. Some of these have a trompe l'oeil effect: the painted window appears to have ivy growing out of it; the bed seems to be sprouting sunflowers.

waking—there are bears on unicycles and storks being tugged along in a chariot. The third mural, an ocean scene, depicts animals on boats, including a bear nimbly climbing a mast. In the background, a whale pokes its tail out of the water.

Albright brought the same playful approach to her daughter's furniture. She transformed a beat-up play table and nursery-school chair by adding painted scenes of picnicking animals. (In a wise move, Albright applied several coats of water-based polyurethane to both pieces in order to protect them from messy crafts projects and to make them easier to clean.) She also transformed the Hitchcock bed, a family piece, although in a different way. Albright admires the work of the Herter brothers, who created furniture in the 1880s, and she paid homage to

these furniture makers by decorating the bed with a Herter-like border of insects and flowers.

Painting her daughter's room was truly a labor of love. Her reward? "Seeing Nicola in bed, talking about the animals on the wall, beaming at her beautiful environment."

ABOVE LEFT: These formerly beat-up-looking pieces—a play table and a nursery-school chair—were transformed by artist Joan Albright, who decorated them with bright patterns and scenes. Layers of water-based urethane protect their surfaces from messy crafts projects and other child-related hazards.

ABOVE RIGHT: This mural detail shows a parade of circus animals, complete with three geese in a rolling vase. A rooster brings up the rear.

BELOW: Artist Joan Albright painted the bureau gold and black, using a pattern that pays homage to the Herter brothers, furniture makers who were active in the late nineteenth century.

RIGHT: This mural features framed, detailed scenes, surrounded by simpler trompe l'oeil backgrounds.

SKIP
A
BEAT

Lily Maslon is a young drummer who loves lavender. Left to her own devices she'd have a whole room in this shade, but her mother sought a compromise, thinking such a room would be too intense. Instead, she had the valance and window trim painted purple and, at the windows, added sheer lavender curtains and a row of multicolored beads. She also added a

This room is for a girl who loves lavender; the rest of the room is done in compatible shades. The canopy bed is swathed in white organza. The patterned bedding includes an appealing mix of colors, including soft shades of yellow, pink, and blue. The floral lamp shade, which was handmade in England, has real pressed pansies embedded in it.

chair and an end table in matching rose-colored wicker and a pinkish red chest of drawers. For storage, "I didn't want the heaviness of a big armoire, so I scattered the shelves on the wall," Lily's mother says. She painted each shelf a different pastel color— lavender, yellow, pink—then arranged them asymmetrically.

Flowers dot the room, from the silk ones on the walls to the ones attached to the mirror that's framed in chartreuse tulle. Fabric roses brighten the corners of the bed canopy, which has netting around its frame and posts. Even Lily's bedside lamp has flowers—real pressed pansies—embedded into its shade.

 ### Rose-Garden Swag Mirror

An ordinary mirror can be draped in fantasy with the addition of a swag of tulle or other sheer material. Fabric roses can be glued onto the fabric or onto the mirror itself. For a less-feminine look, substitute almost anything else for the flowers, from plastic animal figures to trading cards.

OPPOSITE PAGE: The fun of this room lies in its daring colors. The bright red wicker furniture, a mirror draped in chartreuse tulle, and ubiquitous purple accents, from window trim to valances, complement each other nicely.

CLOCKWISE FROM TOP LEFT: This floral lamp shade, which was handmade in England, is embedded with real pressed pansies.

A bright neon clock adds to the eclectic mix.

The materials used elsewhere in the room, such as tulle and flowers, were assembled to transform this mirror.

PLAYTIME

When decorator Sasha Emerson created a room for a two-year-old boy named Cyrus, she chose a blue-and-white color scheme. The chest of drawers, the low bureau, and the rice paper light fixtures in Cyrus's room are all blue and white.

To the basic blue-and-white motif, Emerson added doses of other colors, including red and yellow chairs. She found a child-size 1950s red plastic headboard—complete with an illustration of a pirate and map—at a flea market, cut off the legs, then mounted it on the wall.

This room, which was decorated on a budget, mixes new furniture with flea-market finds.

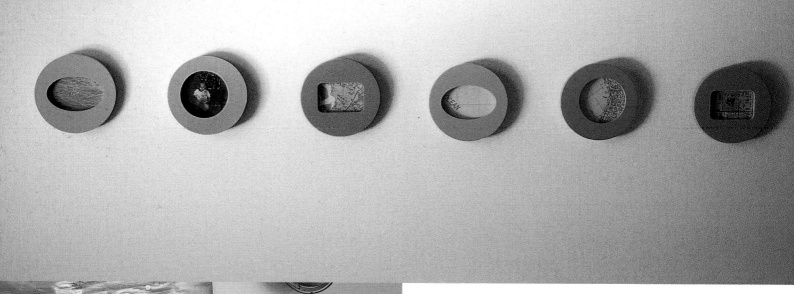

This and other vintage finds, including a timeworn pinball machine and an old, school map of Brazil, brighten the room. The six colorful, round picture frames by the side of bed create a map of a different sort—that of Cyrus's very young life. "They are framed maps and family pictures of places significant to his life," Emerson explains. One holds part of a map of the town where his father grew up; another holds a snippet of a plan of the city where his parents were married. Taken together, they tell his story in terms of the places that formed him, even before he was born.

OPPOSITE, ABOVE: A sequence of small frames tells the story of this boy's young life, including photos of family members and maps of places they've lived.

OPPOSITE, BELOW: A linoleum "carpet" made by Westling Design is both practical and colorful in the play area.

ABOVE: This rolling drawer, which is ideal for toy storage, fits neatly under the bed.

RIGHT: Blue-and-white accents, including a distinctive chest of drawers, unify this room. An old pinball game is flanked by inexpensive—yet stylish—rice-paper-shaded lamps.

SHEER HEAVEN

Ten-year-old Monica Stansbury loves lavender and chartreuse. So when interior designers Jill Wood and Gretchen Gibson, of A Child's Eye View, created a room for this young aspiring actress and dancer, they used copious amounts of these colors. They created a lavish duvet cover that's lavender on one side and chartreuse on the other, and they finished it with a

The girl who lives in this room adores the colors lavender and chartreuse, and she admires the flowing costumes of ballet dancers. Jill Wood and Gretchen Gibson, of A Child's Eye View, chose multicolored sheer swags, scarves, and curtains to create a similar effect.

long fringe. Since they were unable to find a lavender pillow sham, they made one themselves. The window is adorned with yards and yards of multicolored sheer organza, complete with swags in contrasting colors. The cozy window seat—a great place for daydreaming—is enlivened by an assortment of pillows.

ABOVE: An oversized button, in contrasting velvet, adds an elegant touch to this homemade duvet cover.

TOP RIGHT: The soft pillow sham is made in its owner's favorite colors. It can also, of course, be made in other combinations. (See "Organza Pillow Sham," opposite.)

BOTTOM RIGHT: This colorful, fringed duvet cover gives a theatrical flair to a girl's bed.

project: **Organza Pillow Sham**

This sham will cover a standard-size pillow.

1 Cut two pieces from the sheet measuring from finished top edge to 20 inches down and 27 inches wide. Cut a third piece from the sheet, 33 by 27 inches.

2 Sew together the strip of velour to form a loop, and pull the organza through it.

3 Lay the gathered sheer over the 33-by-27-inch piece of the sheet, centering the loop.

4 Fan out the sides of the organza and pin the fanned-out ends to the 27-inch sides.

5 Trim the sheer to match the sheeting, and baste together the two fabrics.

6 To create the back "envelope" of the pillowcase, lay the two back pieces onto the sheer, with right sides facing each other (inside out). Overlap the factory-finished edges in the center by 3 inches to create the envelope for the pillow.

7 Pin and stitch ¼ inch from the edge on all four sides.

8 Turn right side out. Top stitch 2 ½ inches all around to create the flange.

HOOP DREAMS

Zoe's room glows. It has peach-colored walls, a celadon-green bed, and a pale chartreuse armoire that holds books, games, and toys. Zoe, an avid basketball player, is fearless on the court. She's fearless about color, too. So she has a lemon-yellow bedspread, a peach-colored built-in desk and shelves, and a bright red nightstand. The latter is "not a nightstand per se—it's a file drawer," Zoe's mother, Marny Maslon, explains. "Because I was using a day bed, I needed a higher, substantial table to balance the bed." Perched on top of it is an

Slam Dunk. Bold, warm-toned colors, an eye-catching black-board, and original storage solutions make this basketball enthusiast's room an unqualified success.

attention-getting lamp with acrylic flowers that seem to pop out from its base.

There are fun storage solutions here, too. A chalkboard in an animal frame serves both as wall art and as a reminder board. A fabric shoe-holder hangs on the wall—an artful way to display Zoe's Beanie Baby collection, with each creature inhabiting an individual pocket. As for Zoe's passion—basketball—there's an all-important hoop just on the other side of her bedroom door.

LEFT: The pink desk unit incorporates storage and a work surface. On the shelves above are lots of fun distractions from dreary homework.

OPPOSITE, CLOCKWISE FROM TOP LEFT: On an orange-red bedside table sit a flowerpot lamp, a novelty clock, and a pastel-patterned telephone with a peace sign on its dial.

An applique pillow makes Zoe's daybed her own personal space.

Beanie Babies peek out from their ingenious display, a transparent shoe holder.

Discreet shelves are perfect for the display of basketball trophies and books.

resources

Of the many resources listed, some are retail through stores, the Internet, or catalogs, while others are manufacturers. Most stores can handle mail-order, but manufacturers do not sell directly to the public. Instead, manufacturers will tell you the location of the nearest retailer.

FURNITURE

ABC Carpet & Home
888 Broadway
New York, NY 10011
212-473-3000
Beds, tables, chairs, linens, rugs.

Baby Furniture Outlet
270 Adelaide Street South
London, ON N5Z 3L1
Canada
519-649-2590
Cribs, chairs, changing tables.

Baby World of Cambridge
600 Hespeler Road.
Cambridge, ON N1R 8HZ
Canada
519-623-9010
Tables, chairs, rugs, accessories.

Casa Collection Design
79 Bridge Street
Brooklyn, NY 11201
718-694-0272
www.casacollection.com
Manufacturer of children's furniture (call for retail information).

A Child's Place
338-1120 Grant Avenue
Winnipeg, MB
Canada R3M 246
204-284-7633
Children's furniture and accessories.

Crate & Barrel
800-323-5461
www.crateandbarrel.com
Desks, tables, general home furnishings.

Ethan Allen Kids
800-228-9229
www.ethanallen.com
Children's furniture and accessories.

Freedom Furniture
3 Apollo Place
Lane Cove, NSW 2066
Australia
Children's furniture and accessories.

Friendly Bears
10940 Mayfield Road
Edmonton, AB T5P 4B6
Canada
780-489-0707

Friendly Bears Ltd.
103 Princess Avenue
Winnipeg, MB R3B 1K6s
Canada
204-942-1237
Children's furniture and
accessories.

Goodnight Room
5817 College Avenue
Oakland, CA 94618
510-601-6390
Beds, storage, lamps, toys.

IKEA
1-800-434-IKEA
www.ikea.com
Children's furniture and linens.

Kids Supply Co.
1325 Madison Avenue
New York, NY 10128
212-426-1200
Beds, storage, desks, toys.

The Land of Nod
P.O. Box 1404
Wheeling, IL 60090
800-933-9904
www.thelandofnod@aol.com
Catalog specializing in
children's furniture.

Lily Henry Zoe
141 Barrington Place
Los Angeles, CA 90049
310-440-8150
Beds, storage, decorative items.

Maine Cottage Furniture
P.O. Box 935
Yarmouth, ME 04096
207-846-1430
www.mainecottage.com
Children's furniture and
accessories.

Murphy Bed Center
20 West 23rd Street
New York, NY 10010
212-645-7079
www.murphybedcenter.com
Assorted styles of Murphy beds.

Nesting Kids
418 Eglinton Avenue West
Toronto, ON M5N 1A2
Canada
416-322-3356
(Fax) 416-322-3356

Pottery Barn Kids
800-430-7373
www.potterybarn.com
Furniture, rugs, and accessories.

ACCESSORIES

The MoMA Design Store
New York, NY
800-793-3167
OrderService@MoMA.org
Charles and Ray Eames
"Hang-It-All" coat rack.

O.R.E.
1330 Gladys Avenue
Long Beach, CA 90804
562-433-2683
Bulletin boards and magnets.

Putnam Rolling Ladder
32 Howard Street
New York, NY 10013
212-226-5147
Rolling library ladders.

Target
888-304-4000
www.target.com
Lamps, mirrors, and bedding.

FLOORING

ABC Carpet & Home
888 Broadway
New York, NY 10011
212-473-3000
Wide array of floor coverings.

Aronson's Floor Covering Inc.
135 West 17th Street
New York, NY 10011
212-243-4995
Linoleum, rubber floor coverings
in bright colors and patterns.

Forbo Industries
1-800-842-7839
Artofloor, mottled pastel
linoleum panels.

IKEA
800-434-IKEA
www.ikea.com
Hopscotch rug.

Lonseal
800-832-7111
Lonpoint Moonwalk is studded
vinyl, a scaled-down version of
Pirelli rubber flooring, in rolls
of red, yellow, and blue.

Material Connexion
4 Columbus Circle
New York, NY 10019
212-445-8825
Einfo@materialconnexion.com
Colorful interlocking rubber floor
tiles in many colors and textures
like pebbled and hammered.

Wandix International
17 Dicarolis Court
Hackensack, NJ 07601
800-385-6855
201-498-1290
wandix@aol.com
Foam rubber tiles.

LIGHTING

Ad Hoc Softwares
410 West Broadway
New York, NY 10012
212-925-2652
Wide array of lighting fixtures.

Flos
200 McKay Road
Huntington Station, NY 11746
516-549-2745
Philippe Starck's Miss Sissi lamp.

Ingo Maurer
89 Grand Street
New York, NY 10013
212-965-8817
Lamps shaped like wings
and hearts.

Lee's Studio
1755 Broadway
New York, NY 10019
212-581-4400
Light fixtures and lighting
solutions.

Tech Lighting
1718 West Fullerton
Chicago, IL 60614
773-883-6110
www.techlighting.com
Low-voltage halogen lights,
shaped like octopi, biplanes,
and acrobats, which are
suspended from a high-wire.

Tensor Corporation
100 Everett Avenue
Chelsea, MA 02150
617-884-7744
sales@tensorcorp.com
Desk lamps.

STORAGE

Bed Bath & Beyond
800-GO BEYOND
Plastic storage containers.

InterDesign
30725 Solon Industrial Parkway
P.O. Box 39606
Solon, OH 44139
440-248-0178
Plastic bins and baskets.

Kitchen
218 8th Avenue
New York, NY 10011
212-243-4433
Colorful Mexican tote bags,
chili lights—some mail-order
items available.

Romanoff Products
158 5th Avenue
New York, NY 10011
800-828-9587
*www.romanoffproducts@
earthlink.net*
Plastic storage boxes, bins,
buckets.

Winterset Designs
P.O. Box 428
Brattleboro, VT 05302
800-257-5733
Canvas storage bins.

WALLCOVERINGS

Benjamin Moore Paints
800-972-4685
Crayola colors and thousands
of other colors.

Clarence House
211 East 58th Street
New York, NY 10022
212-752-2890
Upscale wallpapers and fabrics.

Greensteel
800-766-4204
Steel covered with a porcelain
coating, so children can draw on
it with washable markers. Can
be used to cover entire walls and
doors, or just a drawing board.

Katzenbach & Warren's
800-974-2466
Wallpapers.

Porters Paints
895 Bourke Street
Waterloo, NSW 2017
Australia
Wide assortment of paint.

Secondhand Rose
138 Duane Street
New York, NY 10013
212-393-9002
Vintage wallpapers.

Helene Verin
21 East 22nd Street
New York, NY 10010
212-533-5525
verin@post.com.
Innovative wallpaper designs.

index